Spiritual Ecology
The Cry of the Earth

A COLLECTION *of* ESSAYS
EDITED *by* LLEWELLYN VAUGHAN-LEE

"Humanity is in the process of evolving to a higher level of consciousness. Our time has come. Over our short and violent history, humanity has traveled a long way down the wrong path. We desperately need to find our way back home before we are forever lost. To make this shift, all who are alive today must learn to live in harmony with the Earth. This book carries urgently needed messages for everyone on the planet. I know this because I have witnessed how damaging human impact is on natural eco-system function and how little time we have left to change this. It is our choice and it is our responsibility to act with courage and wisdom. *Spiritual Ecology* is helping to lead the transition by amplifying the Earth's voice that we so badly need to hear."

JOHN D. LIU, director Environmental Education Media Project, senior research fellow IUCN, and visiting fellow Faculty of Earth and Life Sciences at Vrije University, Amsterdam

"This book takes us beyond—though not around—the grief and despair that the ecological crisis evokes. Herein lies an authentic possibility of healing through a transformation in our own ways of knowing, relating, and being."

CHARLES EISENSTEIN, author *Sacred Economics* and *The Ascent of Humanity*

"This book is a call to action. It requires us to put down everyday concerns that preoccupy our minds and listen with our hearts to the testaments of how desperately the earth needs us. At every moment, our physical, emotional, and spiritual well-being are nurtured by the earth and yet, we are indifferent to this fact as we go about our way pursuing material success. This book is a timely reminder that we must find balance in our lives and give to others as much as we receive from the earth. We must develop compassion for all the living beings that suffer even as we benefit and we must generate courage to make a change in our own behavior. I thank the authors in the book for reinforcing my commitment to protect the earth as much as is in my power."

HIS HOLINESS THE 17TH KARMAPA, OGYEN TRINLEY DORJE

"In many voices, *Spiritual Ecology* speaks a profound and essential truth, inspiring us all to listen to the cry, deepen our personal reflection, and expand the circle of conversation about our connection with Earth and with each other. Our human future depends on recognizing and embracing Earth as a sacred living being, our birth mother, the source of our nurture, and beyond price."

DAVID KORTEN, author *The Great Turning* and
Agenda for a New Economy, and co-founder
and board chair of *YES! Magazine*

"Llewellyn Vaughan-Lee has assembled a gem of a book reflecting the bright inner light from a pantheon of our most luminary visionaries working to heal the Earth, and with it, ourselves. *Spiritual Ecology* elegantly repairs the most fundamental systems error in our relationship with the Earth: the celebration of the sacredness and oneness of all life. For millennia, prophets, mystics and poets have spoken about the oneness of all life. Today biology is confirming that belief with the most basic genetic fact of life: As human beings, we are literally kin with the entire diversity of life, from the microbes to the mammals. This book is a must-read and will elevate your spirit, expand your vision, and nourish your heart."

KENNY AUSUBEL, co-founder of Bioneers and author
Dreaming the Future: Reimagining Civilization in the Age of Nature

"Like life herself, she thrums with the sounds of nature—and this book left me thrumming too. Our natural state is as one when we accord with nature's own laws and when we align our being with nature; that is where we find peace. This book is a step in that journey for us all to find peace."

POLLY HIGGINS, advocate for Earth Law, award-winning
author *Eradicating Ecocide* and *Earth is our Business*,
ecologist and voice for the Earth

"What ails us is deeper than what's easily measurable by economics or science. *Spiritual Ecology* is a collection of profound writings by some of the wisest among us about the depths of the crisis and the wellsprings of redemption."

DAVID W. ORR, Oberlin College, author *Earth in Mind*,
and founder The Oberlin Project

"The collection of essays of renowned spokespeople have a sort of magical property that is a basic call to consciousness of our relationship to our Mother Earth. The messages reflect almost a supernatural quality through the shared knowledge, wisdom and ancient teachings about the importance of the sacred including our place as human beings of which we are only a small part in the cycle of life."

MONA POLACCA, M.S.W., International Council of Thirteen Indigenous Grandmothers and co-secretariat Indigenous World Forum on Water & Peace

"This wonderful anthology of concise but profound essays by scholars and practitioners who are among the foremost pioneers in spiritual ecology ranges widely from African to Zen spiritual traditions as it addresses the ultimate cause of environmental problems from the local to the global levels. That cause is human alienation from nature as nothing but soulless matter for objectification, commodification, and consumption. The ultimate solution is no less than a spiritual re-discovery, re-feeling, and re-connecting with nature as sacred. This skillfully crafted book will prove compelling in its penetrating knowledge and wisdom for university instructors and students from the natural sciences to the humanities, religious and secular professionals, and the general public."

DR. LESLIE E. SPONSEL, author *Spiritual Ecology: A Quiet Revolution*, www.spiritualecology.info

"The environmental crisis is inseparable from the spiritual crisis that exists within the soul of most modern and now post-modern men and women and is in fact an objectivization of this primarily inward crisis. The present volume consists of precious collection of essays by some of the most notable authorities in the field about the essentially spiritual character of the environmental crisis. May the cry of the earth which they describe so vividly in this book be heard far and wide by those who still have ears to hear the truth."

SEYYED HOSSEIN NASR, University Professor of Islamic Studies George Washington University, author *Man and Nature: The Spiritual Crisis of Modern Man*

"This magnificent collection of essays by many of the most respected and prominent voices in the global ecological movement is a rich source of energy, hope and delight in a time when so many of us are overwhelmed by the problems of the planet. They remind us anew of the responsibilities we share, the ideals we must live by, and the ancient and timeless wisdom of the spiritual traditions of all cultures everywhere. This is a book to treasure, to meditate on and to live by."

TOM CHEETHAM, author *All the World an Icon*

"Some of the most inspiring voices on behalf of our living planet speak forth with power and clarity in this hugely important and timely book. Their words help us find our true home and our rightful place within the great turning world of Nature."

STEPHAN HARDING, Ph.D.,
author *Animate Earth: Science, Intuition and Gaia,*
and founding member Schumacher College

"We live in a time of ecological uncertainty and we need opportunities to reconnect with the sacred. Just as scientists are modern-day prophets who tell us why we must act to save our planet, the essayists in this book are sages who remind us why that work is worthwhile."

THE REV. CANON SALLY G. BINGHAM, founder
The Regeneration Project – Interfaith Power & Light

"Time is running out on our ability to manage successfully our impacts on the earth, its environment, biodiversity, resource and life-support systems on which human life as we know it depends. The response and action that is now required of us must be firmly rooted in our deepest moral and spiritual principles. The important collection of voices in this book address this urgent need."

MAURICE STRONG, former Under-Secretary General
of the United Nations and author *Where on Earth Are We Going?*
and co-author *Only One Earth: The Long Road
via Rio to Sustainable Development*

"This book is filled with poetic, poignant, intelligent voices, calling for a fresh and deepened attention to our suffering planet. Listening and responding to the call is itself a path of true awakening—one that reveals our innate belonging to this living world, and the sacredness that shines through all of life."

TARA BRACH, Ph.D., author *Radical Acceptance* and *True Refuge*

"This book is important to the survival of humanity. We must reconnect with Mother Earth and treat her as the source of all life instead of a resource to be plundered. The writers of this book are the real super heroes of our times. They have done the deep work and have come to the point of understanding our true connection to Earth. This is the key to our future if we are to have one. Everyone must read this book, understand it and live it if we are to leave anything to our children and grandchildren."

HANNE STRONG, founder The Manitou Foundation and Earth Restoration Corps

"I am in awe of this magical book, where I recognised with emotion the spirit of a choice I made long ago, in this ancient land of Africa: listen to the songs of the Earth, reconnect with her soul, and by recapturing the reverence for all living things, and the duty to care, find the lost link with hope."

KUKI GALLMANN, author *I Dreamed of Africa* and founder The Gallmann Memorial Foundation, dedicated to the coexistence of people and nature in Africa

"This book responds to the SOS of our planet with a life raft of new thinking, spiritual solace and inspirational calls to action. These essays teach us to both save and savor our resplendent blue and green mothership. I recommend it to all who feel the pain of the world and want to go to work."

MARY PIPHER, author *The Green Boat: Reviving Ourselves in Our Capsized Culture*

"The Earth is sacred. Such is the mantra of this gloriously timeless yet undeniably timely cry of a book."

LAURIE LANE-ZUCKER, executive director Seven Pillars House of Wisdom

"*Spiritual Ecology* is not just an important growing movement to watch, it is *the* critical development of our time.
Environmental Studies, Cultural Studies, and Religious
Studies scholars alike will benefit from this valuable resource for the classroom. Filled with insights from some
of the world's most passionate eco-prophets, this volume's
fascinating contributions all point toward a way into the
future marked by peace and prosperity for the whole life
community. Scholarly yet accessible, *Spiritual Ecology*
was a delight to read, and I know my students will resonate
with it as well."

SARAH MCFARLAND TAYLOR, Ph.D., Associate Professor
of Religious Studies and Environmental Policy
and Culture at Northwestern University

"The voices in this book offer a vital wake-up call, and a
message of urgency and hope. Their vision represents a
sustainable future—environmentally and spiritually."

REV. FLETCHER HARPER, director
GreenFaith, www.greenfaith.org

"There is a transmission that comes through the words of
those willing to be in true intimacy with life in all its agony
and ecstasy, and we need that transmission. We need the
pathways laid by those willing to feel it all, so that we can
follow, feel and find a new way. This book is an anchor pull
back into the poignancy of our own connectedness, via the
gentle tugs and full-hearted calls of the leaders gathered
here. Earth is calling: read this book with an open heart
and you will feel her. ..."

CLARE DAKIN, founder TreeSisters,
www.treesisters.org

"In my scholarly work I have explored our Earth for signs
of life in defense of life. The signs can be found in a host of
social movements around the world, which are inspired by
a growing chorus of passionate voices. This volume provides
direct access to many of these voices, some well known,
others less so, all wise. It belongs in public and university
libraries, the classroom, and wherever activists gather for
inspiration and action."

BRON TAYLOR, author *Dark Green Religion:
Nature Spirituality and the Planetary Future*

Spiritual Ecology

The Cry of the Earth

A COLLECTION *of* ESSAYS
EDITED *by* LLEWELLYN VAUGHAN-LEE

THE GOLDEN SUFI CENTER

First published in the United States in 2013 by
The Golden Sufi Center
P.O. Box 456
Point Reyes, California 94956.
www.goldensufi.org

Fourth printing, 2014

Printed and bound by Thomson-Shore.

ISBN 13: 978-1-890350-46-8 *(hardcover)*
ISBN 13: 978-1-890350-45-1 *(paperback)*

Library of Congress Cataloging-in-Publication Data
Spiritual ecology : the cry of the earth, a collection of essays / edited by
Llewellyn Vaughan-Lee.
    pages cm
  Includes bibliographical references.
  ISBN 978-1-890350-46-8 (hardcover : alk. paper) -- ISBN 978-1-890350-
45-1 (pbk. : alk. paper) -- ISBN 978-1-890350-47-5 (pdf) (print) -- ISBN
978-1-890350-49-9 (kindle) -- ISBN 978-1-890350-53-6 (epub)
  1. Human ecology--Religious aspects. 2. Environmentalism--Religious
aspects. I. Vaughan-Lee, Llewellyn.
  GF80.S667 2013
  201'.77--dc23
                            2013009911

This book is printed on 100% post-consumer recycled paper,
FSC Certified, and processed without chlorine.

Contents

Introduction

THE EARTH is in distress and is calling to us, sending us signs of the extremity of its imbalance through earthquakes and tsunamis, floods and storms, unprecedented heat and drought. There are now indications that its ecosystem as a whole may even be approaching a "tipping point" or "state shift" of irreversible change with unforeseeable consequences.

And some of us are responding to these signs, hearing this calling, individually and as groups, with ideas and actions—trying to bring our collective attention to our unsustainable materialistic lifestyle and the ways it is contributing to ecological devastation, accelerating pollution, species depletion. And yet, sadly, much of this response comes from the same mindset that has caused the imbalance: the belief that we are separate from the world, that it is something "out there," a problem we need to solve.

The world is not a problem to be solved; it is a living being to which we belong. The world is part of our own self and we are a part of its suffering wholeness. Until we go to the root of our image of separateness, there can be no healing. And the deepest part of our separateness from creation lies in our forgetfulness of its sacred nature, which is also our own sacred nature. When our Western monotheistic culture suppressed the many gods and goddesses of creation, cut down the sacred groves and banished God to heaven, we began a cycle that has left us with a world destitute of the sacred, in a way unthinkable to any indigenous people. The natural world and the people who carry its wisdom know that the created world and all of its many inhabitants are sacred and belong together. Our separation from the natural world may have given us the fruits of technology and science, but it has left us bereft of any instinctual connection to the spiritual dimension of life—the connection between our soul and the soul of the world, the knowing that we are all part of one living, spiritual being.

It is this wholeness that is calling to us now, that needs our response. It needs us to return to our own root and root-edness: our relationship to the sacred within creation. Only from the place of sacred wholeness and reverence can we begin the work of healing, of bringing the world back into balance.

This book is a collection of responses to the call of the Earth. Each sounds a different note in response to that call, offers its own way of being attentive, of remembering what is sacred—just as we all need to respond, each in our own way, so that we may once again be present here, holding the Earth within our hearts and souls as well as in our minds and hands.

These responses are not offered as a solution to a problem, because the world is not a problem but a living being in distress. The signs of global imbalance—the tsunamis, the destruction of the coral reefs—are not just physical symptoms. As Thich Nhat Hanh writes, these are "bells of mindfulness," calling us to be attentive, to wake up and listen. The Earth needs our attention. It needs us to help heal its body, damaged by our exploitation, and also its soul, wounded by our desecration, our forgetfulness of its sacred nature. Only when we remember what is sacred can we bring any real awareness to our present predicament.

Each of these chapters can be seen as a different way of describing a journey, one we must make now, from our soulless, materialistic wasteland to a land rich in meaning and sacred purpose, which knows the name and place of all of its myriad inhabitants. On this side, where our world stands now, we each live our separate lives, isolated within our individual, anxious self. On the other side, we feel the patterns of interrelationship that support and nourish us, and can commune together as a single living community; we feel the mystery and magic of a world full of sacred meaning and purpose. It is only when we stand on this other shore that we can hope to heal our world, to help it to become free of this nightmare of materialism that is destroying its fragile and magical beauty. Only then can we return to our ancient heritage as guardians of the Earth.

The chapters of this book offer a range of different perspectives on the awakening needed to make this journey. We hear from Chief Oren Lyons, the Faithkeeper of the Turtle Clan of the Onondaga Nation, whose words carry the authority and knowing of one of the present wisdom-keepers of the land, turning our attention back to the primacy of natural law; from Father Thomas Berry, one of the original voices of much of our present understanding of spiritual ecology, expressing sadness at the failure of the European settlers of North America to recognize the magnificence of the land and the spirituality of its peoples, and voicing our desperate need to regain our sense of wonder and reverence; from Zen Buddhist monk Thich Nhat Hanh, urging us to wake up and look at the signs the Earth is sending us of its distress and to cultivate a new way based on kindness and compassion. We hear a variety of perspectives from the Buddhist, Celtic, Christian, Native American, Persian, Indian, and Sufi traditions; we look through the lens of systems theory, sacred lands, the use of the imagination, the sacredness of food, the world of the archetypes, and a new story of a living intelligent universe. We hear the voices and visions of an African chief, a farmer and beloved poet, a Catholic nun grounded in an earth-based spirituality, a Franciscan monk, an American shaman, an Indian physicist and activist, a wilderness guide, and others as well.

As the editor, I am deeply grateful to all those who have given their voices to this collection of responses to what is a spiritual as well as a physical global crisis. In different ways they all articulate the same message: a need to regain our natural spirituality, the spirit that belongs to nature. Only when our feet learn once again how to walk in a sacred manner, and our hearts hear the real music of creation, can we bring the world back into balance.

And at the same time, between these pages there is also a warning—sometimes articulated, sometimes more hidden. If we remain forgetful of the sacred in all of life and do not redeem our split between spirit and matter, our planet will become more and more out of balance. As its soul is starved of our spiritual connection, life as we know it will begin to fall to pieces and die. This is already beginning to happen in a small way, but we do not know how fast it will accelerate, when we will reach the "tipping point." We urgently need to reclaim our guardianship of the physical and sacred world. We need to remember why we are here. To quote Wendell Berry:

> "The care of the Earth is our most ancient and most worthy, and after all, our most pleasing responsibility. To cherish what remains of it and to foster its renewal, is our only legitimate hope."

—LLEWELLYN VAUGHAN-LEE, *Editor*

Behold, my brothers, the spring has come;
the earth has received the embraces of the sun and
we shall soon see the results of that love!

Every seed has awakened and so has all animal life.
It is through this mysterious power that we too
have our being and we therefore yield to our neighbors,
even our animal neighbors, the same right as
ourselves, to inhabit this land.

TATANKA YOTANKA, SITTING BULL

Faithkeeper of the Turtle Clan of the Onondaga Nation,
CHIEF OREN LYONS *is responsible for maintaining the customs and traditions of his people, while representing their message to the world community. Here he speaks about the spiritual laws of nature and the absolute nature of those laws. We have to change our ways and stop making war against Mother Earth. We need to learn once again how to respect nature, to be thankful and enjoy life.*

Listening to Natural Law
CHIEF OREN LYONS

NEYAWENHA SKANNOH. It means "Thank you for being well." The greeting in itself is something of an idea of how Indian people think and how their communities operate.

What happens to you and what happens to the earth happens to us as well, so we have common interests. We have to somehow try to convince people who are in power to change the direction that they've been taking. We need to take a more responsible direction and to begin dealing with the realities of the future to insure that there *is* a future for the children, for the nation. That's what we're about. It is to our advantage as well as yours to be doing that.

In the concern and in the fights that we face as a common people, as human beings, as a species, we have to get together and we have to do things like we're doing now—meeting, sharing, learning. It all comes down to the will, what is in your heart. Indian people have survived up to this time because we have a strong will. We do not agree that we should be assimilated. We do not agree that we should give up our way of life. And that same will should be in your heart—the will that you do not agree that there be no future.

I don't believe, personally, that we have reached a point of no return in this situation that we're in, but we are approaching it. The farther you're away from a point of no return, the more options you have. As we move each day closer to a point of no return, we lose that day's option. And there will come a point where we won't have an option. There will be no more options. At that point, people will cry and people will carry on and so forth. But as Chief Shenandoah said to me, "I don't know what the big problem is. It's too late anyway." I said, "Uncle, what do you mean by that?" "Well," he says, "they've done a lot of damage. They're going to suffer." Kind of a simple observation, but true enough. There is a lot of damage done and people are going to suffer, but he didn't carry out the thought that we were told a long time ago in the prophecies, that there was going to be a degradation of the earth. We were told that you could tell the extent of the degradation of the earth because there would be two very important systems to warn you.

One would be the acceleration of the winds. We were told that the winds would accelerate and continue to accelerate. When you see that the accelerations of the winds are growing, then you are in dangerous times. They said the other way to tell that the earth was in degradation was how people treated their children. They said it will be very important to note how people treat their children, and that will tell you how the earth is degrading. So when you open up the newspapers today, they talk about exploitive sex and children, they talk about homeless children, and you can count homeless children by the millions. To us, it's a severe indication of the degradation. Society doesn't care.

So we have to take those signposts seriously and begin to organize ourselves and do the best we can. We must gather ourselves together, give ourselves some moral support, enough to go home and start over and do it again, because everything starts at home. It starts right there with you. It starts with you and then your family. Then from your family it goes out, and that's how you do it, that's how you have to do it. It's grassroots. You go back and you begin to inform and you get a little more excited and you get a little more severe in your positions and you begin to insist that people hear and listen. Education is important and how you educate people as to what we need is fundamentally important.

The spiritual side of the natural world is absolute. The laws are absolute. Our instructions—and I'm talking about for all human beings—our instructions are to get along. Understand what these laws are. Get along with laws, and support them and work with them. We were told a long time ago that if you do that, life is endless. It just continues on and on in great cycles of regeneration, great powerful cycles of life regenerating and regenerating and regenerating.

If you want to tinker with that regeneration, if you want to interrupt it, that's your choice, but the results that come back can be very severe, because again, the laws are absolute. There's no habeas corpus in natural law. You either do or you don't. If you don't, you pay. It's quite simple. So what we have to do is get our leaders to change, and if our leaders don't do it, we've got to raise better leaders, newer leaders. Raise your own leaders. Get them up there. It's your responsibility to raise good leaders. Get them up there where they can be effective and change the direction of the way things are headed.

I come from Onondaga, and from our country I remember when everybody planted. I stood behind one of those plows that you hooked behind a horse. And at my age, if you hit a rock, you flew right over the plow handle. It was hard to hold that plow. I remember that. It was hard work. Planting and agriculture are hard work. You have to get up early. You've got to do stuff, but it's great training for character. It's great training for becoming adult and becoming responsible, the best training really. But getting back to agriculture is hard to do these days. There will come a time, however, when only those that know how to plant will be eating.

That's not far off. So all of those Indian Nations that built whole civilizations around food and around thanksgiving and around spiritual law, those Indian Nations have to resurge and have to remind one another how important that is. All communities talk about prayer. We just don't call it prayer, but we do it all the time. We sing songs, dawn songs, morning ceremonies, thanksgiving-coming-up-soon-songs. Thanksgiving all summer, all spring. All of our ceremonies are thanksgiving. We have thanksgiving twelve months a year.

In the spring when the sap runs through the trees, we have ceremonies, thanksgiving. For the maple, chief of the trees, leader of all the trees, thanksgiving. Thanksgiving for all the trees. Planting thanksgiving. Thanksgiving for the strawberries, first fruit. Thanksgiving for the bees, the corn, green corn, thanksgiving. Harvest thanksgiving. Community, process, chiefs, clan mothers, everybody is there. Families are there. How do you inspire respect for something? By giving thanks, by doing it.

We have to do that. We have to be thankful. That's what we said. Two things were told to us: To be thankful, so those are our ceremonies, ceremonies of thanksgiving. We built nations around it, and you can do that, too. And the other thing they said was enjoy life. That's a rule, a law—enjoy life—you're supposed to. I know you can only do as much as you can do, and then when you do that, you're supposed to get outside and enjoy life. Don't take yourself so seriously. Do the best you can but get at it. That's the way you and I have community. I'll be down in the mouth and be moping and dragging around, but by meeting with people and sitting and talking and listening to all of the positive energy and the intentions at Bioneers, for instance, and other gatherings, it's renewable. I can go home and I can say, hey, there is a good bunch of people over there and they're working hard trying to help us out. Tell our own people to get off their lazy asses and do something. It's true. People are lazy today. They don't know how to work anymore.

That's the way it is and that's what it's going to take. Hard work will do anything. It used to be common, common law. So I would say that in the ideas of renewing yourself and the ideas of finding peace in our community, you should tell your leaders and you should tell everybody that there can never be world peace as long as you make war against Mother Earth. To make war against Mother Earth is to destroy and to corrupt, to kill, to poison. When we do that, we will not have peace. The first peace comes with your mother, Mother Earth.

Dahnayto (Now I am finished).

i thank You God for most this amazing
day:for the leaping greenly spirits of trees
and a blue true dream of sky;and for everything
which is natural which is infinite which is yes

E. E. CUMMINGS

THOMAS BERRY, *one of the most influential recent figures in Earth-based spirituality, sees the Earth as the primal source of our spirituality. "If there is no spirituality in the Earth, then there is no spirituality in ourselves." We have forgotten that the revelation found in the natural world and in the wider universe around us is the primary divine revelation. We need to regain the sense of wonder that comes from being deeply interconnected in a sacred way.*

The World of Wonder
THOMAS BERRY

WHAT DO YOU SEE? What do you see when you look up at the sky at night, at the blazing stars against the midnight heavens? What do you see when the dawn breaks over the eastern horizon? What are your thoughts in the fading days of summer as the birds depart on their southward journey, or in the autumn when the leaves turn brown and are blown away? What are your thoughts when you look out over the ocean in the evening? What do you see?

Many earlier peoples saw in these natural phenomena a world beyond ephemeral appearance, an abiding world, a world imaged forth in the wonders of the sun and clouds by day and the stars and planets by night, a world that enfolded the human in some profound manner. This other world was guardian, teacher, healer—the source from which humans were born, nourished, protected, guided, and the destiny to which we returned.

Above all, this world provided the psychic power we humans needed in our moments of crisis. Together with the visible world and the cosmic world, the human world formed a meaningful threefold community of existence. This was most clearly expressed in Confucian thought, where the human was seen as part of a triad with Heaven and Earth. This cosmic world consisted of powers that were dealt with as persons in relationship with the human world. Rituals were established whereby humans could communicate with one another and with the earthly and cosmological powers. Together these formed a single integral community—a universe.

Humans positioned themselves at the center of this universe. Because humans have understood that the universe is centered everywhere, this personal centering could occur anywhere. For example, the native peoples of North America offered the sacred pipe to the powers of the four directions to establish themselves in a sacred space where they entered into a conscious presence with these powers. They would consult the powers for guidance in the hunt, strength in wartime, healing in time of illness, support in decision-making. We see this awareness of a relationship between the human and the powers of the universe expressed in other cultures as well. In India, China, Greece, Egypt, and Rome, pillars were established to delineate a sacred center, which provided a point of reference for human affairs and bound Heaven and Earth together.

There were other rituals whereby human communities validated themselves by seasonal acknowledgement of the various powers of giving ceremony, where the sun, the Earth, the winds, the waters, the trees, and the animals each in turn received expressions of personal gratitude for those gifts that made life possible. Clearly, these peoples see something different from what we see.

We have lost our connection to this other deeper reality of things. Consequently, we now find ourselves on a devastated continent where nothing is holy, nothing is sacred. We no longer have a world of inherent value, no world of wonder, no untouched, unspoiled, unused world. We have *used* everything. By "developing" the planet, we have been reducing Earth to a new type of barrenness. Scientists are telling us that we are in the midst of the sixth extinction period in Earth's history. No such extinction of living forms has occurred since the extinction of the dinosaurs some sixty-five million years ago.

There is now a single issue before us: survival. Not merely physical survival, but survival in a world of fulfillment, survival in a living world, where the violets bloom in the springtime, where the stars shine down in all their mystery, survival in a world of meaning. All other issues dwindle in significance—whether in law, governance, religion, education, economics, medicine, science, or the arts. These are all in disarray because we told ourselves: We know! We understand! We see! In reality what we see, as did our ancestors on this land, is a continent available for exploitation.

When we first arrived on this continent some four centuries ago, we also saw a land where we could escape the monarchical governments of Europe and their world of royalty and subservience. Here before us was a land of abundance, a land where we could own property to use as we wished. As we became free from being ruled over, we became rulers over everything else. We saw the white-pine forests of New England, trees six feet in diameter, as forests ready to be transformed into lumber. We saw meadowland for cultivation and rivers full of countless fish. We saw a continent awaiting exploitation by the chosen people of the world.

When we first arrived as settlers, we saw ourselves as the most religious of peoples, as the most free in our political traditions, the most learned in our universities, the most competent in our technologies, and most prepared to exploit every economic advantage. We saw ourselves as a divine blessing for this continent. In reality, we were a predator people on an innocent continent.

When we think of America's sense of "manifest destiny," we might wish that some sage advice regarding our true role had been given to those Europeans who first arrived on these shores. We might wish that some guidance in becoming a life-enhancing species had been offered during these past four centuries. When we first arrived on the shores of this continent, we had a unique opportunity to adjust ourselves, and the entire course of Western civilization, to a more integral presence to this continent.

Instead, we followed the advice of the Enlightenment philosophers, who urged the control of nature: Francis Bacon (1561–1626), who saw human labor as the only way to give value to the land; René Descartes (1596–1650) and John Locke (1632–1704), who promoted the separation of the conscious self from the world of matter. In 1776, when we proclaimed our Declaration of Independence, we took the advice of Adam Smith's (1723–1790) *Inquiry into the Nature and Causes of the Wealth of Nations,* a book of enormous influence in the world of economics from then until now. Our political independence provided an ideal context for economic dominance over the natural world.

As heirs to the biblical tradition, we believed that the planet belonged to us. We never understood that this continent had its own laws that needed to be obeyed and its own revelatory experience that needed to be understood. We have only recently considered the great community of life here. We still do not feel that we should obey the primordial laws governing this continent, that we should revere every living creature—from the lowliest insect to the great eagle in the sky. We fail to recognize our obligation to bow before the majesty of the mountains and rivers, the forests, the grasslands, the deserts, the coastlands.

The indigenous peoples of this continent tried to teach us the value of the land, but unfortunately we could not understand them, blinded as we were by our dream of manifest destiny. Instead we were scandalized, because they insisted on living simply rather than working industriously. We desired to teach them our ways, never thinking that they could teach us theirs. Although we constantly depended on the peoples living here to guide us in establishing our settlements, we never saw ourselves as entering into a sacred land, a sacred space. We never experienced this land as they did—as a living presence not primarily to be used but to be revered and communed with.

René Descartes taught us that there was no living principle in the singing of the wood thrush or the loping gait of the wolf or the mother bear cuddling her young. There was no living principle in the peregrine falcon as it soared through the vast spaces of the heavens. There was nothing to be communed with, nothing to be revered. The honeybee was only a mechanism that gathered nectar in the flower and transformed it into honey for the sustenance of the hive, and the maple tree only a means for delivering sap. In the words of a renowned scientist: "For all our imagination, fecundity, and power, we are no more than communities of bacteria, modular manifestations of the nucleated cell."[1]

In order to counter reductionistic and mechanistic views of the universe such as this, we need to recover our vision, our ability to see. In the opening paragraph of *The Human Phenomenon*, Pierre Teilhard de Chardin (1881–1955) tells us: "One could say that the whole of life lies in seeing. That is probably why the history of the living world can be reduced to the elaboration of ever more perfect eyes…. See or perish. This is the situation imposed on every element of the universe by the mysterious gift of existence."[2] We need to begin to see the whole of this land. To see this continent, we might imagine ourselves in the great central valley that lies between the Appalachian Mountains to the east and the Rocky Mountains to the west. Here we would be amazed at the vast Mississippi River, which flows down through this valley and then on into the immense gulf that borders the southern shores of this continent. This massive flow of water, including its tributary the Missouri, flowing in from the northwest, constitutes one of the greatest river systems on the planet, draining almost the entire continent, from New York and the Appalachian Mountains in the east to Montana and the Rocky Mountains in the west.

This region includes the Great Plains, the tall grasslands that extend from Indiana to the Mississippi River, to the short grasslands that begin across the river and extend to the mountains. This is a territory to be honored in some special manner. The region to the west of the river has what are among the deepest and most fertile soils on the planet. Soils that elsewhere are only inches in depth here are several feet deep, soils formed of the debris washed down from the mountains over long centuries. A large human population depends on this region. Such precious soil is a gift to be carefully tended. This center of commercial wheat, and later corn production, began in New York in the early nineteenth century and extended westward until now it can be located in those Kansas fields of grain that extend beyond the horizon.

When we stand in the Mississippi basin, we can turn westward and experience the mystery, adventure, and promise of this continent; we can turn eastward and feel its history, political dominance, and commercial concerns. Westward are the soaring redwoods, the sequoia, the Douglas fir, the lodgepole pine; eastward are the oaks, the beech, the sycamore, the maple, the spruce, the tulip poplar, the hemlock. Together, these bear witness to the wonder of the continent and the all-encompassing sea.

We might also go to the desert, or high in the mountains, or to the seashores, where we might really see, perhaps for the first time, the dawn appear in the eastern sky—its first faint purple glow spreading over the horizon, then the slow emergence of the great golden sphere. In the evening, we might see the flaming sunset in the west. We might see the stars come down from the distant heavens and present themselves almost within reach of our arms if we stood on tiptoe.

So too, we might begin to view the change of the seasons: the springtime awakening of the land as the daisies bloom in the meadows and the dogwood tree puts forth its frail white blossoms. We might experience the terrifying moments when summer storms break over the horizon and lightning streaks across the sky, the moments when darkness envelops us in the deep woodlands, or when we experience the world about us as a vast array of powers asserting themselves. When we view all this, we might begin to imagine our way into the future.

Concerning this future we might make two observations. First, the planet Earth is a onetime project. There is no real second chance. Much can be healed because the planet has extensive, albeit limited, powers of recovery. The North American continent will never again be what it once was. The manner in which we have devastated the continent has never before occurred. In prior extinctions, the land itself remained capable of transformations, but these are now much more difficult to effect. Second, we have so intruded ourselves and debilitated the continent in its primordial powers that it can no longer proceed simply on its own. We must be involved in the future of the continent in some comprehensive manner.

It is clear that there will be little development of life here in the future if we do not protect and foster the living forms of this continent. To do this, a change must occur deep in our souls. We need our technologies, but this is beyond technology. Our technologies have betrayed us. This is a numinous venture, a work of the wilderness. We need a transformation such as the conservationist Aldo Leopold (1887–1948) experienced when he saw the dying fire in the eyes of a wolf he had shot. From that time on, he began to see the devastation that we were bringing upon this continent. We need to awaken, as did Leopold, to the wilderness itself as a source of a new vitality for its own existence. For it is the wild that is creative. As we are told by Henry David Thoreau (1817–1862), "In Wildness is the preservation of the world."[3] The communion that comes through these experiences of the wild, where we sense something present and daunting, stunning in its beauty, is beyond comprehension in its reality, but it points to the holy, the sacred.

The universe is the supreme manifestation of the sacred. This notion is fundamental to establishing a cosmos, an intelligible manner of understanding the universe or even any part of the universe. That is why the story of the origin of things was experienced as a supremely nourishing principle, as a primordial maternal principle, or as the Great Mother, in the earliest phases of human consciousness. Some of the indigenous peoples of this country experience it as the Corn Mother or as Spider Woman. Those who revere the Corn Mother place an ear of corn with the infant in the cradle to provide the soothing and security the infant needs to feel deep in its being. From the moment the infant emerges from the warmth and security of the womb into the chill and changing world of life, the ear of corn is a sacred presence, a blessing.

We must remember that it is not only the human world that is held securely in this sacred enfoldment but the entire planet. We need this security, this presence throughout our lives. The sacred is that which evokes the depths of wonder. We may know some things, but really we know only the shadow of things. We go to the sea at night and stand along the shore. We listen to the urgent roll of the waves reaching ever higher until they reach their limits and can go no farther, then return to an inward peace until the moon calls again for their presence on these shores.

So it is with a fulfilling vision that we may attain—for a brief moment. Then it is gone, only to return again in the deepening awareness of a presence that holds all things together.

Every day, priests minutely examine the Law
and endlessly chant complicated sutras.
Before doing that, though, they should learn
how to read the love letters sent by the wind
and rain, the snow and moon.

Iκκυ

Zen Buddhist monk, poet, and peace activist THICH NHAT HANH *urges us to wake up from the dream that is destroying the planet. Our mindfulness can change our collective consciousness, giving us the power to decide the destiny of our planet.*

The Bells of Mindfulness
THICH NHAT HANH

The bells of mindfulness are calling out to us,
trying to wake us up, reminding us to look
deeply at our impact on the planet.

THE BELLS OF MINDFULNESS are sounding. All over the Earth, we are experiencing floods, droughts, and massive wildfires. Sea ice is melting in the Arctic and hurricanes and heat waves are killing thousands. The forests are fast disappearing, the deserts are growing, species are becoming extinct every day, and yet we continue to consume, ignoring the ringing bells.

All of us know that our beautiful green planet is in danger. Our way of walking on the Earth has a great influence on animals and plants. Yet we act as if our daily lives have nothing to do with the condition of the world. We are like sleepwalkers, not knowing what we are doing or where we are heading. Whether we can wake up or not depends on whether we can walk mindfully on our Mother Earth. The future of all life, including our own, depends on our mindful steps. We have to hear the bells of mindfulness that are sounding all across our planet. We have to start learning how to live in a way that a future will be possible for our children and our grandchildren.

I have sat with the Buddha for a long time and consulted him about the issue of global warming, and the teaching of the Buddha is very clear. If we continue to live as we have been living, consuming without a thought of the future, destroying our forests and emitting dangerous amounts of carbon dioxide, then devastating climate change is inevitable. Much of our ecosystem will be destroyed. Sea levels will rise and coastal cities will be inundated, forcing hundreds of millions of refugees from their homes, creating wars and outbreaks of infectious disease.

We need a kind of collective awakening. There are among us men and women who are awakened, but it's not enough; most people are still sleeping. We have constructed a system we can't control. It imposes itself on us, and we become its slaves and victims. For most of us who want to have a house, a car, a refrigerator, a television, and so on, we must sacrifice our time and our lives in exchange. We are constantly under the pressure of time. In former times, we could afford three hours to drink one cup of tea, enjoying the company of our friends in a serene and spiritual atmosphere. We could organize a party to celebrate the blossoming of one orchid in our garden. But today we can no longer afford these things. We say that time is money. We have created a society in which the rich become richer and the poor become poorer, and in which we are so caught up in our own immediate problems that we cannot afford to be aware of what is going on with the rest of the human family or our planet Earth. In my mind I see a group of chickens in a cage disputing over a few seeds of grain, unaware that in a few hours they will all be killed.

People in China, India, Vietnam, and other developing countries are still dreaming the "American dream," as if that dream were the ultimate goal of mankind—everyone has to have a car, a bank account, a cell phone, a television set of their own. In twenty-five years the population of China will be 1.5 billion people, and if each of them wants to drive their own car, China will need 99 million barrels of oil every day. But world production today is only 84 million barrels per day. So the American dream is not possible for the people of China, India, or Vietnam. The American dream is no longer even possible for the Americans. We can't continue to live like this. It's not a sustainable economy.

We have to have another dream: the dream of brotherhood and sisterhood, of loving kindness and compassion. That dream is possible right here and now. We have the *Dharma*, we have the means, and we have enough wisdom to be able to live this dream. Mindfulness is at the heart of awakening, of enlightenment. We practice breathing to be able to be here in the present moment so that we can recognize what is happening in us and around us. If what's happening inside us is despair, we have to recognize that and act right away. We may not want to confront that mental formation, but it's a reality, and we have to recognize it in order to transform it.

We don't have to sink into despair about global warming; we can act. If we just sign a petition and forget about it, it won't help much. Urgent action must be taken at the individual and the collective levels. We all have a great desire to be able to live in peace and to have environmental sustainability. What most of us don't yet have are concrete ways of making our commitment to sustainable living a reality in our daily lives. We haven't organized ourselves. We can't only blame our governments and corporations for the chemicals that pollute our drinking water, for the violence in our neighborhoods, for the wars that destroy so many lives. It's time for each of us to wake up and take action in our own lives.

We witness violence, corruption, and destruction all around us. We all know that the laws we have in place aren't strong enough to control the superstition, cruelty, and abuses of power that we see daily. Only faith and determination can keep us from falling into deep despair.

Buddhism is the strongest form of humanism we have. It can help us learn to live with responsibility, compassion, and loving kindness. Every Buddhist practitioner should be a protector of the environment. We have the power to decide the destiny of our planet. If we awaken to our true situation, there will be a change in our collective consciousness. We have to do something to wake people up. We have to help the Buddha to wake up the people who are living in a dream.

Now in the people that were meant to be green there is no more life of any kind. There is only shriveled barrenness. The winds are burdened by the utterly awful stink of evil, selfish goings-on. Thunderstorms menace. The air belches out the filthy uncleanliness of the peoples. The earth should not be injured! The earth must not be destroyed!!

HILDEGARD VON BINGEN

At a gathering of the Global Peace Initiative of Women in Kenya, CHIEF TAMALE BWOYA, *a traditional Chief from the Buganda Kingdom in Uganda, shared a dream he had the previous night. It revealed that the fate of the Earth was hanging in the balance, and that to continue with negative actions would destroy life on Earth. He was told in the dream that those who had gathered from all over the world represented the new "chiefs" who held the sacred responsibility for healing and saving the Earth at this critical time.*

Revelation at Laikipia, Kenya
CHIEF TAMALE BWOYA

ON 4 MARCH 2012 at about 3:00AM, I, Chief Tamale Bwoya, was awakened by a voice that said, *"Wake up Chief."* I woke up and sat on the bed inside the tent I was sleeping in.

Nature opened up its screen. On the screen, I saw a panel of judgment. There in the dock sat men of all races as they seem to be on earth, and each of them was dressed in a uniform manner but with distinctive colors, waiting for judgment. (These men were a blueprint of the men on earth and were directly responsible and accountable for the mistakes of men they respectively stood for on earth.)

The voice spoke again, *"The world was put in the hands of the chiefs, but you failed in your work. Can you guarantee now that humanity is ready to rehabilitate its relationship with nature?"*

Inside me, it seemed very difficult to change the way people behaved towards natural life. The destruction of the plant kingdom, the animal kingdom, and the entire ecosystem, through modernization, scientific inventions, social and political greed, hatred, etc. I could not answer; instead tears started flowing down my eyes. Deep inside me, I felt guilty of human actions and mistakes.

The men occupied the same space in the dock and were given everything in equal proportions, opportunities and judgment. Very interestingly, the mistake of a particular race was adding up to the total of human mistakes on a water-base-scale, and humanity was to be condemned in totality, not in single units. The judgment panel and its people were at a higher level, and the earth was far below, appearing to be in semi-darkness. On the left-hand side, there were women all dressed in ice-white (like the Indian sisters we were with who are based in Kenya) but without anything covering their heads. These women were very busy and very fast recording and filling. It appeared as if they were recording human works on earth, and the scores were automatically reflecting on the water-base-scale.

The water-base-scale automatically registers all human activities, both positive and negative, and the effect of each race could directly change the level of water-base regardless of the race (whether caused by Africans, Indians, Europeans, etc.).

The water-base-scale was registering human performance in totality (positive + negative = change on scale). The water-base-scale has an overflowing point, which if ever reached and water overflows, even by a single drop, would automatically activate an invisible, potentially enormous force above the men on the panel of judgment that would dissolve humanity with all the wildlife. It is at this point that man will have condemned himself to dissolution through his own actions irrespective of whether any of the races did better or the other destroyed nature more—all humanity will dissolve beginning with the men on the panel of judgment, and the world will follow with all the wildlife that was put under human supervision and care.

At this point the world will be cleansed of all the badness, bloodstain, hatred, etc. Mountains and non-living materials on earth will not be condemned together with man. Instead all will automatically return to their original forms and places. Man will just dissolve away and all will disappear in thin air. There will be no more cars or skyscrapers to be seen. No nuclear bases, or shuttles, or airplanes to be seen on earth anymore. The world will go back to its original form. All wildlife and man-made objects will go with him.

On the water-base-scale there remained very little space to reach the overflowing point. It appeared that if man maintains the pace at which he destroys the environment (nature), within very few years humanity will be no more. The only chance was that if man changes his ways today, in respect to nature and environment, the water-base will automatically drop, giving humanity a bigger chance.

After a moment of silence, I asked, *"Who are the chiefs?"* (since I was told by the voice in the beginning that the world was put in the hands of the chiefs). I was shown a pictorial message of all the men and women from all over the world that gathered at Laikipia Natural Conservancy in a group, and the voice spoke again, *"Those are the chiefs of your generation."*

After a moment of silence, I saw nature closing its screen, and after some time I laid on my bed ready to sleep, though deeply in thoughts. The voice spoke again. *"That message is not for you; record it, you have to tell them."*

I woke up and recorded the message using a small torch.[1]

Give me a heart
I can pour out in thanksgiving.
Give me life
So I can spend it
Working for the salvation of the world.

SHEIKH ANSARI OF HERAT

JOHN STANLEY & DAVID LOY *combine scientific realism with the ecological message of engaged Buddhism, pointing to a new story for our Earth that has love and connection at its center.*

At the Edge of the Roof:
The Evolutionary Crisis of the Human Spirit
JOHN STANLEY & DAVID LOY

We have constructed a system we can't control. It imposes itself on us, and we become its slaves and victims. We have created a society in which the rich become richer and the poor become poorer, and in which we are so caught up in our own immediate problems that we cannot afford to be aware of what is going on with the rest of the human family or our planet Earth. In my mind I see a group of chickens in a cage disputing over a few seeds of grain, unaware that in a few hours they will all be killed.

—THICH NHAT HANH

SINCE PALAEOLITHIC TIMES, indigenous human cultures have maintained rituals that express a sacred relationship to the living world. Why did these spiritual-ecological instincts have survival value for our ancestors? Why is it so difficult to get in touch with them in modern society? Why has it become so difficult for our species to remember that we come from nature, are dependent on it and return to it?

Spontaneous affinity with the natural world is our natural state. It is still evident in the fascination and delight of children with plants and animals of all kinds, an appreciation not limited to young people of course. There is a link between a love of nature, deep spiritual experience and our moral sense. It is a key part of the human spirit. It can leave us lost for words.

By using the words *spirit* and *spiritual*, we are not referring to a religious belief system or to anything supernatural. We are referring to the fact that we are spiritual animals. After Darwin, it is no longer possible for anyone (except religious fundamentalists) to ignore our biological evolutionary lineage. We are human primates. We are the dominant animal on Earth. We are also spiritual beings having a human experience.

So why did the "human empire" arrive at such an alarming state of ecological overshoot? An obvious and dismaying fact is that our so-called leaders—or rulers—will not agree to do what it takes to make the future livable. Meanwhile, we are left uninformed by the corporate media about scientific truths or solutions. Advertising sells us the notion that the answer involves more technology and hedonism. It inflames hyper-individualism to such an extent that community and society seem to be breaking down. In this all-too-human dilemma, the poet Rumi's advice has never seemed more pertinent:

> Sit, be still, and listen,
> For you are drunk,
> And we are at the edge of the roof.

A DIVIDED BRAIN & ITS CONSEQUENCES

The intuitive mind is a sacred gift, and the rational mind is a faithful servant. We have created a world that honors the servant, but has forgotten the gift.

—ALBERT EINSTEIN

In *The Master and his Emissary*, neurological psychologist Iain McGilchrist presents a wealth of scientific evidence that these two realities are rooted in the bi-hemispheric structure of our brain. The cerebral hemispheres are specialized and each has motor control of the opposite side of the body. In the 250,000-year history of *Homo sapiens*, they have had a long history of productive co-evolution. The inclusive and empathic right hemisphere is attuned to intuition, empathy, relationship and creativity. The left hemisphere gives us linguistic consciousness (re-presentation of life in words), mathematics and control of the dominant hand from which arose the making of complex tools.

McGilchrist suggests that the evolutionary relationship between our right and left hemispheres resembles the tale of a wise spiritual master who selflessly rules a kingdom. Seeing that it is not possible for him to personally supervise the bureaucracy of government in distant parts of his realm, the master entrusts that to his brightest emissary. As time goes by, however, the ambitious emissary prioritizes his own goals and values. Finally he gains sufficient power and position to dupe the people and imprison the master. The outcome is a tyranny that eventually leads to collapse and ruin.

An inner power struggle between these hemispheres can be inferred in Western history. This led to a comprehensive triumph for left-hemisphere verbal thinking, computation and technology. It produced the so-called Enlightenment, Newtonian physics and the coal-driven Industrial Revolution.

We now live in the world the left hemisphere has built, replacing the ancient Soul of the World (*Anima Mundi*) with its own mechanistic model. Its preoccupation with competition and control has been institutionalized. It has become our way of life. The right hemisphere's concern for empathic relationship and a broader vision has been marginalized. We could understand the twentieth century as the left hemisphere's project to build a planetary empire. It did so through an industrial growth-economy powered by oil, advertising and consumerism. This one-sided ambition for power and profit has proved so intoxicating that we now find ourselves "at the edge of the roof."

The difference between the two brain hemispheres invites comparison with a distinction in Asian spiritual traditions between small self and big Self. For example, Mahayana Buddhism and Advaita Vedanta both distinguish our usual limiting ego-self from an unlimited "original self." Ego-self is characterized by what Einstein called the "optical illusion of separateness." But we do not have to be stuck with it. In fact the key point of the evolutionary crisis of the human spirit is that we can no longer afford to be limited by it. Fortunately, the ego-self can be re-trained, to develop a more inclusive identity. I am more than me. I am connected to you. I am a member of we.

When we meditate in a completely engaged way, we lose the sense of time. Then the brain creates new neural networks. Both the functioning and the structure of the brain change. To a real-time brain-scanning instrument, those changes appear as greater harmonic complexity. Biological evolution happens in real time as a reflection of spiritual evolution.

These discoveries have important implications for all who follow a path of personal transformation. This is also the case for the social transformation that is necessary if civilization is to come safely down to earth from "the edge of the roof." We have to come to the realization that our original self includes the whole living world. That kind of empathy, based on a holistic worldview, is essential. Without it we will not survive the ecological and social "great unraveling" that has already begun.

CLIMATE CHANGES EVERYTHING

> *If six degrees centigrade of global warming takes place, 95% of species will die out, including Homo sapiens. Mass extinction has already happened five times and this is the sixth. According to the Buddhist tradition there is no birth and no death—after extinction things will appear in other forms. So you have to breathe very deeply in order to acknowledge the fact that we humans may disappear from this Earth in just one hundred years. You have to learn how to accept that hard fact, without being overwhelmed by despair. That is why we have to learn to touch eternity in the present moment, with our in-breath and out-breath.*
>
> —THICH NHAT HANH

In 2012 the world crossed an ominous threshold. A reading of 400 parts per million (ppm) of atmospheric carbon dioxide was recorded by monitoring stations across the Arctic. That is at least 50ppm higher than the maximum concentration during the last 12,000 years, a period that allowed us to develop agriculture and civilization. It was also a year in which the Arctic sea-ice melted in summer to some 55% of its 1990 extent, and America was engulfed by a massive and prolonged drought that destroyed much of its wheat and soybean crops. In other words, chaotic climate change became a "new normal."

With respect to the Arctic, in particular, the senior British climatologist Peter Wadhams of Cambridge University has warned that the north polar ice cap is likely to disappear in summer by 2016—decades ahead of mainstream projections. Temperature rises in the Arctic could then trigger "positive feedback" cycles, like the melting of Siberian permafrost, releasing ancient methane. Such a powerful new source of greenhouse gas could constitute a tipping point for the global climate. Thich Nhat Hanh is correct: progression to six degrees centigrade of global warming can no longer be ruled out.

Collusion between the corporate media and fossil fuel industry is a well-concealed triumph of propaganda. It is devastating agriculture on a global scale. Mary Robinson and Desmond Tutu among others have pointed out that poor people in the Third World have been suffering such effects for years, and called for "climate justice." It is now obvious that ongoing climate impacts on agriculture will continue to worsen worldwide. The composition of the atmosphere affects rich and poor countries alike. What a stable climate gives, global warming takes away: first agriculture, then civilization.

A natural conviction held by every previous human generation is that *our children are our future*. How can this advanced globalized society sleepwalk into an unprecedented betrayal of inter-generational justice? We need to ask ourselves: in whose interest are we sacrificing the ancient contract with the future of our species? Why can't we find the courage to face the facts, and throw off the dominion of the fossil fuel industry? That kind of authentic challenge would re-invigorate the human spirit.

The great biologist Edward Wilson concludes that three major traits, resulting from our evolutionary heritage, define the character of our species. Natural selection within a group favored self-concern. But natural selection between groups favored the empathic traits of cooperation and altruism. They serve the human spirit and our remarkable social intelligence. Within the individual and within society, struggles between these instinctive behaviors are inevitable. All societies have therefore developed rules for socialization that inhibit or channel self-centeredness. However, the old religious symbolisms that used to constrain human greed and aggression cannot compete with the hi-tech advertising industry. By glorifying self-concern as never before, consumerism generates a mental environment of endless competition. It undermines empathy, altruism and cooperation.

Yet humans are the most social of animals. Our altruistic instinct is so strong that it has created large, highly valued niches for its expression, such as medicine, education and other helping professions. Altruistic activity is one of the most potent factors that can strengthen a person's immune system and boost longevity. No wonder we honor self-sacrifice for the group with great ceremony. Altruism and cooperation are two key survival factors for our species.

Climate chaos represents an enormous threat to a host of human rights: the right to food, water and sanitation, to social and economic development. It has recently been suggested that human rights courts should treat climate change as an immediate threat to our rights. They could impose a duty to cooperate on the basis of the Universal Declaration of Human Rights. Governments would be required to end their corrupt relationship with fossil fuel corporations. They would have to commit to build a post-carbon society at the scale and tempo of a war effort. This can be based on the fact that professional engineering bodies all over the world have confirmed we already have all the technology we need. Because climate changes everything, the global emergency requires that a new article be added to the Declaration, specifying the human right to a safe climate.

The dominant institution of our age is no longer religion, government or academia. It is the global business corporation. Well-documented examples of corporate behavior correspond to traits of psychopathy, a condition of zero-empathy with others. Of course, not all corporations act as if they were functional psychopaths. Yet the record shows that leading fossil fuel companies possess a truly dangerous combination of wealth, power and destructive intent. They spend huge sums of money to undermine climate science, subvert political institutions and corrupt governments. Where can we find the power to dismantle such a systemic problem? Thom Hartmann and many others have suggested that corporate charters should be revoked and rewritten. Why should delinquent corporations have a legal charter to make enormous profits by destroying the public good and the planet?

Evolutionary biology equipped us with altruism, cooperation and moral being as special resources to expand the range of self-concern. This is how we can address a bigger picture. That picture now concerns the survival of all complex life forms on Earth.

THE UNIVERSE IS AN EVOLUTIONARY PROCESS

The Universe is the only self-referential reality in the phenomenal world. It is the only text without context.
—THOMAS BERRY

Most religions are uncomfortable with evolution, because it seems incompatible with their own creation stories, especially when those stories are understood literally. But if religions are to remain relevant today, they need to embrace biological evolution and focus on its spiritual dimension and meaning.

Most scientists also have a limiting belief: scientific materialism. There has been a power struggle between this particular dogma and authoritarian religion for hundreds of years. The resulting culture war is one of the sideshows that confuse our real quandary. In the face of an unprecedented crisis of biological extinction—including the very real possibility of the disappearance of our own species—we need to put meaning and spirit back into the scientific model. Humanity today deserves a deeper truth to live for than either religion or science has provided alone.

If we look up at night, the space between the stars seems black, but radio telescopes reveal that it contains a faint background glow—cosmic microwave background radiation. This is the primordial light released when the universe exploded into being at the time of the Big Bang. That radiation survives as a cosmic relic, because the universe has been expanding since its origin about 13.7 billion years ago.

Our universe is an evolutionary process. It gives rise to progressively greater levels of complexity, from atoms to stars and solar systems, and finally to a unique planet like ours, which can produce a whole living world. Isn't this amazing? Here on Earth, we have the biological evolution of diverse ecosystems, millions of species and innumerable individual life forms. Our own species has developed cultural evolution. A special case of cultural evolution is the development of excellence, creativity, mastery and wisdom—qualities found in highly evolved humans such as Buddha, Bach, Gandhi or Einstein.

The global ecological crisis is also the defining spiritual crisis of the human species. We are being challenged as a species, to "grow up or get out of the way." Our old social patterns have pitted personal well-being against that of others. The self-interest of the nation state still supersedes the collective well-being of humanity, as every global summit that purports to be concerned with humanity's future confirms. Meanwhile, the new reality of ecological overshoot exposes how radically interdependent we are with the whole living world. All kinds of old stories of our separation from the natural world have brought us to where we are now.

The challenge is to create a new story that brings together the best of science with the best of the non-dual spiritual traditions—Buddhism, Advaita Vedanta, Taoism, Sufism and other mystical traditions. By looking deeper than the duality of a God who created the universe, deeper than the duality of a *nirvana* to which we can escape from earthly *samsara*, and deeper than the duality of scientific materialism, we recognize that the universe is a self-aware creative process.

This pure creative potentiality is in us too. It can awaken and free itself from the limiting identities and games of the human condition.

At the edge of the roof, we need to be exquisitely mindful. We need to know our values. That makes for clarity and good decisions. Zen master Thich Nhat Hanh coined the term *Engaged Buddhism*. He points out that love and connection are the heart of spiritual ecology:

> When we recognize the virtues, the talent, the beauty of Mother Earth, something is born in us, some kind of connection—love is born. We want to be connected. That is the meaning of love, to be at one.... You would do anything for the benefit of the Earth, and the Earth will do anything for your well-being.

Everything you see has its roots
In the unseen world.
The forms may change
Yet the essence remains the same.
Every wondrous sight will vanish,
Every sweet word will fade,
But do not be disheartened,
The Source they come from is Eternal,
Growing, branching out,
Giving new life and new joy.
Why do you weep?
That Source is within you
And this whole world
Is springing up from it.
The Source is full,
Its waters are ever-flowing;
Do not grieve,
Drink your fill!
Don't think it will ever run dry,
This is the endless Ocean.

RUMI

Author and scholar MARY EVELYN TUCKER *and mathematical cosmologist* BRIAN THOMAS SWIMME *focus on the role of humanity in the unfolding story of Earth and cosmos. Our present crisis belongs to a transition into a new consciousness of our place in this story. Waking up to our fundamental relationship with the cosmos and the Earth will help us to take responsibility for our shared future.*

The Next Transition:
The Evolution of Humanity's Role in the Universe

MARY EVELYN TUCKER
& BRIAN THOMAS SWIMME

AS WE SEE our present interconnected global challenges of widespread environmental degradation, climate change, crippling poverty, social inequities, and unrestrained militarism, we know that the obstacles to the flourishing of life's ecosystems and to genuine sustainable development are considerable.

In the midst of these formidable challenges, in an era that Paul Crutzen has dubbed the Anthropocene,[1] we are being called to the next stage of evolutionary history. This new era requires a change of consciousness and values—an expansion of our worldviews and ethics. The evolutionary life impulse moves us forward from viewing ourselves as isolated individuals and competing nation states to realizing our collective presence as a species with a common origin story and shared destiny. The human community has the capacity now to realize our intrinsic unity in the midst of enormous diversity. And, most especially, we have the opportunity to see this unity as arising from the dynamics of the evolutionary process itself. In the 150 years since Darwin's *On the Origin of Species*, we have been developing—for the first time—a scientific story of the evolution of the universe and earth.[2,3] We are still discovering the larger meaning of the story, namely, our profound connectedness to this process.

With the first photograph of earth from space in 1966 came a new and emerging sense of belonging to the planet. In addition, our growing knowledge of evolution continues to give us an expanded sense of the whole. We are beginning to feel ourselves embraced by the evolutionary powers unfolding over time into forms of ever-greater complexity and consciousness. The elements of our bodies and of all life forms emerged from the explosions of supernovas. We are realizing, too, that evolution moves forward with transitions, such as the movement from inorganic matter to organic life and from single-celled organisms to plants and animals, that sweep through the evolutionary unfolding of the universe, the earth, and humanity. All such transitions come at times of crisis, they involve tremendous cost, and they result in new forms of creativity. The central reality of our times is that we are in such a transition moment.

Surrounding this moment is an awakening to a new consciousness that is challenging older paradigms of the human as an isolated being in a random, purposeless universe. Paul Raskin of the Tellus Institute has called this the Great Transition,[4] while the deep ecologist and systems thinker Joanna Macy has named it the Great Turning.[5] Many such thinkers are suggesting that our consciousness is gradually shifting from valuing hyperindividualism and independence to embracing interdependence and kinship on a vast scale. This will take time, but the ecological sciences are showing us the interconnectedness of life systems. The Enlightenment values of life, liberty, and the pursuit of happiness are being reconfigured. Life now includes the larger life of the earth, individual freedom requires responsibility to community, and happiness is being defined as more than material goods.[6] A sense of a larger common good is emerging: the future of the planet and its fragile biosphere.

In this spirit we are moving from an era dominated by competing nation states to one that is birthing a sustainable multicultural planetary civilization. Such a transition, while marked by struggle and conflict, is occurring within the context of our emerging understanding of the Journey of the Universe.[7] The thousands of organizations dedicated to reconfiguring sustainability are an indicator of this shift. And these organizations are coming into being at every level, from the international and national to the bioregional and local, as Paul Hawken describes in his book *Blessed Unrest*.[8]

THE COSMOLOGICAL CONTEXT:
EVOLUTION & EXTINCTION

Over the past century, the various branches of science have begun to weave together the story of a historical cosmos that emerged some 13.7 billion years ago. This has been called the Epic of Evolution by E. O. Wilson[9] and Cosmic Evolution by Eric Chaisson.[10] The magnitude of this universe story is beginning to dawn on humans as we awaken to a realization of the vastness and complexity of this unfolding process.

At the same time that this story is becoming available to the human community, we are becoming conscious of the multidimensional environmental crisis and of the rapid species and habitat destruction taking place around the planet.[11] Just as we are realizing the vast expanse of time over which the universe has evolved, we are recognizing how late is our arrival in this stupendous process. Just as we are becoming conscious that earth took more than 4 billion years to bring forth this abundance of life, it is dawning on us how quickly we are foreshortening its future flourishing.

We need, then, to step back to assimilate our cosmological context. If scientific cosmology gives us an understanding of the origins and unfolding of the universe, philosophical reflection on scientific cosmology gives us a sense of our place in the universe. And if we are so radically affecting the story by extinguishing other life forms and destroying our own nest, what does this imply about our ethical sensibilities or our sense of the sacred? As science is revealing to us the particular intricacy of the web of life, we realize we are unraveling it, although unwittingly in part. Until recently we have not been fully conscious of the deleterious consequences of our drive toward economic progress and rapid industrialization.

As we begin to glimpse how deeply embedded we are in complex ecosystems, and how dependent on other life forms, we see we are destroying the very basis of our continuity as a species. As biology demonstrates a fuller picture of the unfolding of diverse species in evolution and the distinctive niche of species in ecosystems, we are questioning our own niche in the evolutionary process. As the size and scale of the environmental crisis is more widely grasped, we are seeing our own connection to this destruction. We have become a planetary presence that is not always benign.

THE AMERICAN MUSEUM OF NATURAL HISTORY:
UNIVERSE & EARTH EVOLUTION

This simultaneous bifocal recognition of our cosmological context and our environmental crisis is clearly demonstrated at the American Museum of Natural History in New York with two major permanent exhibits. One is the Rose Center that houses the Hall of the Universe and the Hall of the Earth. The other exhibit is the Hall of Biodiversity.

The Hall of the Universe is architecturally striking. It is housed in a monumental glass cube, in the center of which is a globe containing the planetarium. Suspended in space around the globe are the planets of our solar system. In a fascinating mingling of inner and outer worlds, our solar system is juxtaposed against the garden plaza and street scenes of New York visible through the soaring glass panels of the cube. After first passing through a simulation of the originating fireball, visitors move onto an elevated spiral pathway. The sweeping pathway ushers visitors into a descending walk through time that traces the 12 billion-year-old cosmic journey from the great flaring forth in the fireball, through the formation of galaxies, and finally to the emergence of our solar system and planet. It ends with the evolution of life in the Cenozoic period of the last 65 million years and concludes with one human hair under a circle of glass, with the hairsbreadth representing all of human history. The dramatic effect is stunning as we are called to reimage the human in the midst of such unfathomable immensities.

The Hall of Earth reveals the remarkable processes of the birth of earth; the evolution of the supercontinent, Pangaea; the formation of the individual continents; and the eventual emergence of life. It demonstrates the intricacy of plate tectonics, which was not widely accepted even 50 years ago, and it displays geothermal life forms around deep-sea vents, which were only discovered a decade ago. This exhibit, then, illustrates how new our knowledge of the evolution of the earth is and how much has been discovered within the last century.

In contrast to the vast scope of evolutionary processes evident in the Hall of the Universe and the Hall of the Earth, the Hall of Biodiversity displays the extraordinary range of life forms that the planet has birthed. A panoply of animals, fish, birds, reptiles, and insects engages the visitor. A plaque in the exhibit observes that we are now living in the midst of a sixth-extinction period due to the current massive loss of species. It notes that, while the five earlier periods of extinction were caused by a variety of factors, including meteor collisions and climate change, humans are, in large part, the cause of this present extinction spasm.

With this realization, not only does our role as a species come into question, but our viability as a species remains in doubt. Along with those who recognized the enormity of the explosion of the atomic bombs in Japan, we are the first generations of humans to actually imagine our own destruction as a species.

The exhibition notes, however, that we can stem this tide of loss of species and habitat. The visitor walks through an arresting series of pictures and statistics that record the current destruction on one side and that highlight restoration processes on the other. The contrasting displays suggest that the choice is ours: to become a healing or a deleterious presence on the planet.

These powerful exhibits on cosmic evolution and on species extinction illustrate how science is helping us to enter into a macrophase understanding of the universe and of ourselves as a species among other species on a finite planet. The fact that the Rose Center is presenting the evolution of the universe and the earth as an unfolding story in which humans participate is striking in itself. Indeed, the introductory video to the Hall of the Universe observes that we are "citizens of the universe," born out of stardust and the evolution of galaxies, and that we are now responsible for its continuity. In addition, the fact that the Hall of Biodiversity suggests that humans can assist in stemming the current extinction event is a bold step for an "objective" and "unbiased" science-based museum.

Scientists are no longer standing completely apart from what they are studying. They are assisting us in witnessing the ineffable beauty and complexity of life and its emergence over billions of years. They are pointing toward a more integrative understanding of the role of the human in the midst of an extinction cycle. Some of this shift in the museum's perspective arose in the late 1990s when the curators were searching for an ornithologist. Of the final six candidates, four of them had had their birds go extinct while they were studying them. This was alarming to the museum curators, who realized they could not simply stand by and witness extinction with disinterested objectivity.

It can be said, then, that this new macrophase dimension of science involves three intersecting phases: understanding the story of the universe with the best scientific methods, integrating the story as a whole (cosmic, earth, human), and reflecting on the story with a sense of our responsibility for its continuity.

Environmental ethicists and scholars of the world's religions are also being called to contribute to this large-scale macrophase understanding of the universe story. The challenge for religion and ethics is both to re-vision our role as citizens of the universe and to reinvent our niche as members of the earth community. This requires reexamining such cosmological questions as where we have come from and where we are going. In other words, it necessitates rethinking our role as humans within the larger context of universe evolution as well as in the closer context of natural processes of life on earth. What is humankind in relation to 13.7 billion years of universe history? What is our place in the framework of 4.6 billion years of earth history? How can we foster the stability and integrity of life processes? These are critical questions underlying the new consciousness of the universe story. This is not simply a dynamic narrative of evolution; it is a transformative cosmological story that engages human energy for a future that is sustaining and sustainable.

COSMOLOGICAL STORIES

Since the earliest expressions of human culture, humans have struggled to understand and define our place in the universe.

We have developed cosmologies, which are stories that describe where we have come from and where we are going. The religious and cultural traditions we have honored for millennia all bear witness to our deep desire to find meaning in what we see and feel around us.

Over the last two centuries, however, the scientific paradigm has taken root and, in many cases, has become the dominant worldview. Through the scientific method, science tends to objectivize what it describes. In recent years, scientific and religious cosmologies have therefore coexisted uneasily. Some scientists and philosophers have come to the conclusion that the universe, while appearing to follow certain natural laws, is largely a random and accidental accretion of objects, with little meaning and certainly no larger purpose. Scientific facts are separate from human values. One of the aims of the Journey of the Universe perspective is to counteract this view with a presentation of a dynamic and creative universe. Relying on the best of modern science, we discover how we are part of this ongoing journey and now are shaping its future form. This can be an important context for ecological, economic, and social transformation on behalf of our emerging planetary community.

THE GOAL: PROVIDING AN INTEGRATING STORY

The goal of the Journey of the Universe is to tell the story of cosmic and earth evolution, drawing on the latest scientific knowledge in a way that makes it both relevant and moving. What emerges is an intensely poetic story that evokes emotions of awe and excitement, fear and joy, belonging and responsibility.

This universe story is a dramatic one. Throughout billions of years of evolution, triumph and disaster have been only a hairsbreadth apart. Violence and creativity are pervasive.

The ability of matter to organize and reorganize itself is remarkable—from the formation of the first atoms to the emergence of life. We are coming to realize that the energy released at the very beginning has finally, in the human, become capable of reflecting on and exploring its own journey of change. Simple hydrogen has become a vibrant living planet, with beings that now are able to investigate how this has happened and to imagine a life-sustaining future.

Waking up to our fundamental relationship with the cosmos will be a means of reengagement with life. The Journey of the Universe enables us to connect more deeply with the universe and the earth of which we are a part. In doing this, we will appreciate the need for a sustainable human presence on the planet.

Thus the integrated story of the origin and development of the universe, of earth, and of humans could become an inspiring vision for our time.[12] This is because this story is giving us a sense of common evolutionary heritage and shared genetic lineage. This new understanding of the kinship we share with each other and with all life could establish the foundations for rediscovering our past and sustaining the future.

We can be inspired by this scientific view of nested interdependence—from galaxies and stars to planets and ecosystems—so that we sense how personally we are woven into the fabric of life. We are part of this ongoing journey. From this perspective we can see that our current destructive habits toward the environment are unsustainable. In an evolutionary framework the damage we are causing is immense—indeed, cataclysmic. We can thus recognize ecological, economic, and social change as not only necessary but inevitable. But this will require expanding our frame of reference and broadening our worldview. We are already in the process of doing this as we create the foundations for a sustainable future.

*We are talking only to ourselves. We are not talking
to the rivers, we are not listening to the wind and stars.
We have broken the great conversation. By breaking
that conversation we have shattered the universe.
All the disasters that are happening now are a
consequence of that spiritual "autism."*

THOMAS BERRY,
The Dream of the Earth

SISTER MIRIAM'S *work at Genesis Farm continues in the Earth-centered tradition of Thomas Berry. She is one of the foremost interpreters of his cosmological story of our place in the Universe—what it means to embody this new understanding of being human. She also speaks of a need to make our spirituality practical, knowing that our story is part of the story of the Earth.*

The Work of Genesis Farm:
Interview with
SISTER MIRIAM MACGILLIS

LLEWELLYN VAUGHAN-LEE: Much ecological work only focuses on the physical dimension of our present ecological crisis, but you speak about the Earth in its inner psychic spiritual dimension. Could you articulate what you mean by this, and how it relates to this pressing situation?

SISTER MIRIAM: Yes, I'll try. My understanding of this comes directly out of the work of Thomas Berry, and then out of the further development of these ideas through the work of Brian Swimme and Mary Evelyn Tucker and other scientists and writers. The psychic spiritual dimension of the Universe was expressed in Thomas Berry's piece, *Twelve Principles for Understanding the Universe and the Role of the Human*. It states that there was never a moment in the Universe when there was not a spiritual psychic aspect present. This spiritual psychic aspect has been evolving along with the physical complexity of the Universe—the galaxies, stars, solar system, Earth, life, human life, and human consciousness. The human psyche and human spirit are not some addition to the Universe, but have emerged out of the Universe itself.

Mathematical cosmologist Brian Swimme describes the beautiful dynamics present in the first few seconds of the Universe and how the conditions of its rapid cooling and expansion set up structures that have guided evolution over

13.8 billion years. He shows that if the rate of the expansion had been even fractionally faster, the Universe would have exploded; fractionally slower and it would have imploded.

This means that the Universe is one with itself, throughout its expansion in space and through all of its changes in time. It's a single *unity*; you might say a single acting self. So whatever shows up in the process of emerging into greater and greater creativity and complexity has to be an activity of the Universe itself. And if that's so—and I hold this to be fundamental—then the *unity of the whole* becomes foundational for our understanding. So if, for example, Llewellyn shows up 13 billion years later and realizes that the crisis of the planet in its ecological manifestation needs a spiritual basis, then that's the Universe as Earth in Llewellyn making that observation.

So you can see why a clear emphasis on cosmology is so important. Human beings always ask about the deeper meanings of things. From our earliest experiences of life, we have asked questions such as: *What is the world? Where did it come from? Where is it going? Why is it the way it is? Who am I? Where are we? Why do we die? What is death?* These are the questions people have been asking throughout our history. And as humans we create our answers; they're not dropped in as an illumination from somewhere else. The answers that people create are very directly related to the outer world in which they live: the geography, the place, the forms, the light, the events, the experiences they're having. All these things help to shape their answers to why things are the way they are, and that's what we mean by cosmology. So the Earth's human cultures and cosmologies can be extremely different from one another.

One of the aspects Thomas Berry is so clear about in his description of Western origin stories—and why it has meant so much to me growing up within those stories—is the sense, conveyed in the book of Genesis, that God's original intention was a perfect garden, a state of perpetual bliss. This belief held that in the beginning there was no death or suffering, no negative anything, and that was the original divine intention. But human experience was certainly not like that. The world was full of suffering and violence ... children died, and locusts came in and destroyed the crops.... So why were these things happening?

Thomas Berry suggests that this understanding rests on the notion of a divine being who was *perfect* and *transcendent*. So people might ask, "How could a divine, perfect, transcendent being create a world that has sorrow, death, suffering, and illness?" The Judeo-Christian answer is that the original world must have been different—must have been perfect, like its Creator—and that "something" happened to it. What we're experiencing now, a world where children die and locusts come, is *abnormal*. Normal was the garden, the state of bliss.

And the "something" that happened, in this explanation, is that the original world was changed by the infidelity of the first parents. But just as importantly, the original world was made of matter, so it didn't participate in the transcendent part of God's nature. In the Genesis story, even though the world is described as *good*, God directly breathes a transcendent soul into Adam. This soul—the spirit, the psyche—is a direct infusion of spirit from the transcendent divine Creator. But the rest of the world doesn't get one. So there's the origin of the break. Thomas Berry would describe it as a "radical discontinuity of the human from the other-than-human world."

So if the divine is not in matter—if it's transcendent—then how can humans make a meaningful life? How to recreate happiness? How to make a better world? We can see Western civilization's answer in how we define progress and development and how it drives us to perfect the "fallen" natural world. We redesign it, reengineer it, and attempt to bring it back closer to our idea of its original state, a state of perfection and perpetual bliss. Both Berry and Swimme remark that Disney World is the reflection of these deep unconscious drives.

One other thing about Western cosmology and its development in both Judaism and Christianity is the sense of a millennial vision. This vision anticipates a divine intervention, a promise that in some future time the original state of perfection will be restored. So this human yearning for an end to the conditions of suffering and struggle that mark the present order will end. Then the Earth will "pass away" and there will be a new heaven and a new Earth and the original state of bliss will be restored. But people can't bring it about; only the transcendent can do that. Since the transcendent is taking an awful long time to do it, humans keep up their efforts to create Disney World.

LVL: But your understanding in the new cosmology is that everything in us, even our spiritual understanding, is an expression of the Universe—is actually within the spiritual body of the Universe.

SISTER MIRIAM: Yes, the new cosmology says that the Universe is the source of all its activity. If spirit is present, this is a dimension of the Universe. Earth takes this to a whole new dimension of life and self-aware consciousness in its human expression. The human is participating in this realm of spirit in a far deeper dimension. But the human has to be rooted in the whole and a dimension of the whole.

LVL: What do you think has been the effect of our denial of the sacred in creation, coming from this Judeo-Christian story—how has that affected creation itself? We can see how it's been an outer disaster in the ecological devastation—but how has it affected this interior spiritual nature of creation itself, what you call its deep spiritual interior?

SISTER MIRIAM: As humans we are always hungering for a meaningful wholeness, a fullness that would embrace life as it's really given—with chaos, destruction, death and sickness and suffering, as much a normal dimension of it as happiness, health, beauty, love, and joy. Instead, our beliefs have tended to teach us that pain is a punishment and it's abnormal; or it's temporary, but that we should get over it because the world is going to end and we're going to get the perfect world back again. It won't be this Earth as it is now. Thomas Berry points to this deep, deep psychic drive within the Western psyche and how it tries to fill a vast empty part of ourselves with meaningless pursuits. Typically the religious meanings we hold are still based on our separation from nature—the pursuit of God is equally separated from nature—and so they do not bring us to *truly* reverence nature. We don't go out into our backyard and kneel down before the soil and know that we are in the face of sacred mystery. It's just dirt to us; it's opaque. It's real estate. Whoever has the deed to it *owns* it.

LVL: I think what you say is very important. You've talked about this wasteland, and my sense for a long while is that we've created an inner wasteland as much as an outer wasteland.

SISTER MIRIAM: Right, they mirror each other. Exactly.

LVL: And yet we have to regain this sense of what Thomas Berry talks about, this mystery, this wonder at creation.

SISTER MIRIAM: Yes. And what he's saying, I think, is that you're not going to get this reverent experience only through traditional religion if this original tradition never really had it within its cosmological roots. I think Western religious traditions can give you a wonderful sense of the sacred in the transcendent realm, and in the sacredness of how humans ought to treat one another. But I don't think they're capable at this moment of giving us a sense of a deep spirituality and ethic embedded in the natural world or in the Universe. Because the original story never embedded spirit within it.

But once you begin to discover the Universe as the Universe really has emerged, and if you hold a religious belief that God is the origin, then it is possible to see that what has come forth from God has to be a *sacred revelation*. Once you begin to grasp something of the Universe as *the process by which* God created, then the Universe becomes, as Berry suggests, a *primary* sacred revelation. Earth becomes a *primary* revelation, a *primary* sacred scripture.

LVL: The Sufis actually say, "Wheresoever you turn, there is the face of God."

SISTER MIRIAM: Yes.

LVL: And so how can we recreate an understanding of the world as a place of revelation?

SISTER MIRIAM: Well, I think Thomas and Brian are saying that we won't get this without understanding the Universe itself. That's the primary text, the primary sacred scripture. This hasn't been emphasized in our religious traditions. This clarity is coming to us through science. We've come to know it through observation made available through the powerful scientific instruments that have expanded the range of our sense perceptions. Now, we can be stunned by the beauty and wisdom of what we're contemplating.

LVL: And yet at the same time, we don't seem to have much of an understanding of its deep spiritual interior.

Sister Miriam: Because it's not taught that way. It's not being interpreted that way. The very few scientists who are doing this deep work often don't have the academic freedom to just *know* for the sake of *knowing*, to *contemplate* for the sake of *contemplating*. So much support for scientists is controlled by being employed by some organization, usually a corporation that wants research done for its own economic self-interest.

LVL: What do you see as the greatest obstacles to us returning to this awareness of the sacred within creation—of its mystery, its wonder?

Sister Miriam: Lack of understanding of the evolutionary story, in its fullness—not just as a random or determined physical, meaningless evolution, but as a creative process from the very beginning.

LVL: That has an intelligence within it?

Sister Miriam: Yes. It has a self-organizing capacity, which is ultimately mysterious. We can't define that; nobody sees it. It calls for a different kind of faith and a great humility. But it certainly shatters the earlier concepts that have held our tradition together for thousands of years.

LVL: So we have to be prepared to have our whole conceptual framework shattered or broken open.

Sister Miriam: Yes. And we need people to help interpret that.

LVL: And how do you express this vision in your work at Genesis Farm? How do you communicate it in the very tangible work you do, with the land, with the earth, with the seeds?

Sister Miriam: By the seat of our pants! We don't have any recipe book or road map for doing this, so we sort of go by instinct. For instance, this land we inhabit was given as a gift to my Congregation of Dominican Sisters. One of the first things we did was to put it into preservation so that it would be safe from development. So even if the Dominican Sisters were to lose this land, it's deed-restricted and the state holds that conservation easement, that covenant. It can't become a mall or a condo; it has to remain in farming and open space. So that's one way. If somebody gave you sacred texts to hold in your library, you would make sure they weren't subject to being violated—so that's an analogy.

Some twenty-plus years ago, we also dedicated a section of the land here to the *wild*, saying, "Humans are not permitted here." It's a sanctuary. It's going to be left alone—we are not mature enough to go there. Let it be what it wants to be and it will reveal itself. And a hundred, two hundred years from now, who knows what will be there? The idea was to constrain our inquisitiveness and our need to control it, or even to know it.

And so these things seem simple. We've also marked the equinoxes and solstices for thirty years here. As humans who are part of this land, we honor our unity with all the community of life as we circle the Sun at a particular moment in time. Whether we are entering into the phase of springtime renewal or summer ripeness, autumn inwardness or winter pregnancy, we just keep doing it.

LVL: And does that go together with the cycles of planting and harvesting?

Sister Miriam: They go together with those cycles, but those cycles of cultivation and harvesting are recent human experiences. Before that it was just what Earth was doing, the forests, the seas, the animals, the birds, the microbes, the waters. We're trying to be as primary as we can in that relationship.

LVL: So the people that come to you are reminded of those primal cycles within the Earth and within themselves. Reconnected back to those earlier cycles within Earth?

SISTER MIRIAM: Yes. Because that is the true endowment we carry in the collective consciousness of our human species, and it's written into the DNA of our bodies, even though we're not usually aware of that. But it's written into the DNA and memory of every single creature on this land. We carry that memory. We try to recover the memory of the whole inside ourselves—reconnect with that phenomenon. And it's sacred in its nature. Totally, totally sacred.

And then we have a little garden where we plant old varieties of seeds that have never been hybridized. The planet's seeds are in terrible danger, and we're just a very, very small part of a global movement in great alarm over what is happening to seeds. Not only through hybridization—which has accelerated because all the tiny local seed companies have been bought by huge corporations—but far more alarming because more and more companies like Monsanto are buying up the seed stock of the planet and then manipulating them and patenting them and claiming ownership of them.

And then there's genetic engineering of seeds and animals and all of life, which is a basic violation of the DNA memory. It's very real—it's happening. Monsanto has patents on all kinds of seeds and has manipulated government and government policies to give them the right to plant these seeds everywhere. Their pollen then moves out into the commons: the air, the water, the soil. The birds pick it up. The bees pick it up and transfer it unknowingly to the rest of the plants.

Our work is to help people understand the sacramental aspect of seeds, this primary revelation of the sacred in seeds. When you think of how many generations of plants have adapted to a place as members of an ecosystem over eons of time—before humans—and have creatively worked their way into that community of all beings and have both given themselves to it and been nourished by it—this is a primary sacred community. It's the primary source of a region's health, its sustainability, its ability to regenerate. When humans came into that community, just a blink of an eye ago, and thought that nature was just stuff that's here for us to use and manipulate, we began unraveling this unbelievable legacy called life. So I would say that the whole technology of genetically engineering life—forcing species, through a violent process, to take on characteristics of other species, something which would never ever happen without human interference—is blasphemy, it's sacrilege; it gets at the core of—I don't like the word evil but…. It's a desecration. Every aspect of it is a desecration.

So saving the seeds, protecting them, trying to create a sanctuary where they are a little bit safe is one thing. Then there's the work we do in our educational programs, to help people understand that.

LVL: And a need to reclaim the primary sacred within our ecosystem.

SISTER MIRIAM: Right. Because I really do believe that when we understand the Universe story, it's self-evident that you wouldn't engineer seeds. When we don't understand, then resisting genetic engineering becomes just one more issue among a multitude of issues, and we're constantly putting out fires. So many people are stretched to the limit just putting out fires in these ecological crises. But it's clear that we have to change the fundamental mindset under the system that would do all this. We are challenged to change and transform our basic Western, industrial mindset. This is huge …

LVL: But that means a new vision that is not a return to Eden, doesn't it? We can't go back to that pristine land, but somehow we, as a global culture, have to take a step into a new vision that can reclaim the sanctity of the land and its true nature, which can also support us physically.

SISTER MIRIAM: Yes. It's all one. It's all one. The problem is that some humans think we are separate from everything else, that nature is just given to us to use till we get to where we're really going, which is heaven.

LVL: Which is not in this world.

SISTER MIRIAM: Right.

LVL: So that takes me to another question, about seeking guidance by awakening our inner consciousness. You suggest that the whole Universe, including our planet, has an interior spiritual dimension that is not completely unconscious—there is guidance there, an unfolding meaning. When you talk about awakening our inner unconsciousness, how does this relate to what one might call the inner consciousness of life?

SISTER MIRIAM: Well, I'm trying to figure that out, but I'm also trying to move that way. I think we need to engage two things: We need the rational, analytical, reasoning consciousness that has been developed over eons through human history—the love of knowledge, the love of wisdom really. We need to understand how things work, and how we got here, and how it happened—that's why the story of the Universe is probably the largest context for figuring that out.

. At the same time, we need to be faithful to the deep intuitive inner knowing that is part of the interiority of the whole—of our individual lives, our genealogy, our traditions,

71

and the different traditions of the whole human species, of the whole Earth—of the whole Universe, because it's one seamless interior, which we're also participating in.

LVL: So do you believe that there is a guiding principle within life itself that can help us out of this ecological crisis?

SISTER MIRIAM: I think there is an inherent wisdom—it's obvious at every level of the Universe; but I don't understand it, and I would be reluctant to define or limit it to any one idea or image. I try to avoid objectifying it. I'm just trying to *trust* it.

LVL: That's very important. To trust something greater than ourselves in this unfolding disaster that we're trying to heal.

SISTER MIRIAM: Yes. We've come this far. Why would we not trust what has brought all this forth? Why would we need more than that?

LVL: And what do you see as the role of grace?

SISTER MIRIAM: The whole thing is grace. Everything of the Universe—everything that has brought forth the carbon in my body, my body itself, the trees that are shining outside my window, the bees that are flying around collecting pollen—it's all grace if we recognize it. It's there for us.

LVL: And we are part of it.

SISTER MIRIAM: Right.

LVL: And finally, Sister Miriam, in a talk you gave in 1986 about the fate of the Earth, you expressed some of the ideas that you've expressed just now. I was wondering how you personally see the fate of the Earth now, over twenty-five years later.

SISTER MIRIAM: I don't know what is going to happen. It's a great sorrow. Letting the pain of this into one's psyche—it's a lot, it's a lot …

LVL: You mean the pain of our ecological devastation, of how we're treating the Earth?

SISTER MIRIAM: And what we're doing to each other; and whether we can possibly wake up in time? These kinds of questions are all-consuming, because you can't fix it. You just do your little part—and you've got to be very, very humble and realize that there are limitations. And yet the love that I experience for life—I just want it to go on. I want it to go on. That's all I care about.

LVL: And if you wanted to share something that people could do to help in this reclaiming the sacred, this reconnecting to the mystery of life, is there any advice you could give?

SISTER MIRIAM: Well, there is no one answer for everybody, but I do think each of us at our core longs to matter. More deeply than anything, we want our lives to matter. And to matter, we need to be making a contribution towards the whole. Our culture doesn't help you interpret that except in very few ways. So to me, the identity issue, the identity of who I am—the authentic person—is core to all of this, and I'm not sure in this moment that we can understand that at the depth needed without the Universe story.

LVL: You mean that we are part of the Universe—we have to reclaim our knowing as part of the Universe for our lives to have meaning.

SISTER MIRIAM: Yes. Then it opens up our personal meaning and we matter. It really matters that we exist. Not to be shoppers or professionals or this-that-and-the-other—those things are secondary; but what really matters is this deep, deep, deep identity and meaning.

LVL: So what you are saying is that we have to reclaim our deeper knowing that we are part of the oneness of creation, of the world?

SISTER MIRIAM: Yes. And a part of this time when the Earth is going through terrible devastation, which is being caused by the society, and culture, and a way of life we are all implicated in. We're not redeemed out of this. We're implicit, we're in it.

LVL: Right, we're in it, yet we have to reclaim the wholeness, which for earlier cultures was a perfectly natural way of living.

SISTER MIRIAM: So we need all the wisdom, all the support we can get. We need each other, we need the past. We need the whole. We also need this capacity to see that the present moment is not the final word, that there is always the possibility that we can transcend our own limitations—the planet, the Earth, the society can do that. It's possible to believe that, and work toward it. That's all we can do.

LVL: And can we also believe in the greater wisdom of the Earth—of the Universe?

SISTER MIRIAM: Yes. It hasn't abandoned us.

A fish cannot drown in water,
A bird does not fall in air.
In the fire of creation,
God doesn't vanish:
The fire brightens.
Each creature God made
Must live in its own true nature;
How could I resist my nature,
That lives for oneness with God?

MECHTHILD OF MAGDEBURG

The master of many literary genres, WENDELL BERRY *is at heart a traditionalist, a farmer who uses horses to work his land, and organic fertilizer and pest control. His message is that humans must learn to live in harmony with the natural rhythms of the Earth or perish. In the natural world everything knows its place: here we find "an old intelligence of the heart."*

Contributions from
WENDELL BERRY

I TAKE LITERALLY the statement in the Gospel of John that God loves the world. I believe that the world was created and approved by love, that it subsists, coheres, and endures by love, and that, insofar as it is redeemable, it can be redeemed only by love. I believe that divine love, incarnate and indwelling in the world, summons the world always toward wholeness, which ultimately is reconciliation and atonement with God.

EXCERPT FROM
Another Turn of the Crank[1]

Some Further Words

LET ME BE PLAIN with you, dear reader.
I am an old-fashioned man. I like
the world of nature despite its mortal
dangers. I like the domestic world
of humans, so long as it pays its debts
to the natural world, and keeps its bounds.
I like the promise of Heaven. My purpose
is a language that can repay just thanks
and honor for those gifts, a tongue
set free from fashionable lies.

Neither this world nor any of its places
is an "environment." And a house
for sale is not a "home." Economics
is not "science," nor "information" knowledge.
A knave with a degree is a knave. A fool
in a public office is not a "leader."
A rich thief is a thief. And the ghost
of Arthur Moore, who taught me Chaucer,
returns in the night to say again:
"Let me tell you something, boy.
An intellectual whore is a whore."

The world is babbled to pieces after
the divorce of things from their names.
Ceaseless preparation for war
is not peace. Health is not procured
by sale of medication, or purity
by the addition of poison. Science
at the bidding of the corporations

is knowledge reduced to merchandise;
it is a whoredom of the mind,
and so is the art that calls this "progress."
So is the cowardice that calls it "inevitable."

I think the issues of "identity" mostly
are poppycock. We are what we have done,
which includes our promises, includes
our hopes, but promises first. I know
a "fetus" is a human child.
I loved my children from the time
they were conceived, having loved
their mother, who loved them
from the time they were conceived
and before. Who are we to say
the world did not begin in love?

I would like to die in love as I was born,
and as myself, of life impoverished, go
into the love all flesh begins
and ends in. I don't like machines,
which are neither mortal nor immortal,
though I am constrained to use them.
(Thus the age perfects its clench.)
Some day they will be gone, and that
will be a glad and a holy day.
I mean the dire machines that run
by burning the world's body and
its breath. When I see an airplane
fuming through the once-pure sky

or a vehicle of the outer space
with its little inner space
imitating a star at night, I say,
"Get out of there!" as I would speak
to a fox or a thief in the henhouse.

When I hear the stock market has fallen,
I say, "Long live gravity! Long live
stupidity, error, and greed in the palaces
of fantasy capitalism!" I think
an economy should be based on thrift,
on taking care of things, not on theft,
usury, seduction, waste, and ruin.

My purpose is a language that can make us whole,
though mortal, ignorant, and small.
The world is whole beyond human knowing.
The body's life is its own, untouched
by the little clockwork of explanation.
I approve of death, when it comes in time
to the old. I don't want to live
on mortal terms forever, or survive
an hour as a cooling stew of pieces
of other people. I don't believe that life
or knowledge can be given by machines.
The machine economy has set afire
the household of the human soul,
and all the creatures are burning within it.

"Intellectual property" names
the deed by which the mind is bought
and sold, the world enslaved. We
who do not own ourselves, being free,

own by theft what belongs to God,
to the living world, and equally
to us all. Or how can we own a part
of what we only can possess entirely?
Life is a gift we have
only by giving it back again.
Let us agree: "the laborer is worthy
of his hire," but he cannot own what he knows,
which must be freely told, or labor
dies with the laborer. The farmer
is worthy of the harvest made
in time, but he must leave the light
by which he planted, grew, and reaped,
the seed immortal in mortality,
freely to the time to come. The land
too he keeps by giving it up,
as the thinker receives and gives a thought,
as the singer sings in the common air.

I don't believe that "scientific genius"
in its naive assertions of power
is equal either to nature or
to human culture. Its thoughtless invasions
of the nuclei of atoms and cells
and this world's every habitation
have not brought us to the light
but sent us wandering farther through
the dark. Nor do I believe
"artistic genius" is the possession
of any artist. No one has made
the art by which one makes the works
of art. Each one who speaks speaks
as a convocation. We live as councils

of ghosts. It is not "human genius"
that makes us human, but an old love,
an old intelligence of the heart
we gather to us from the world,
from the creatures; from the angels
of inspiration, from the dead—
an intelligence merely nonexistent
to those who do not have it, but
to those who have it more dear than life.

And just as tenderly to be known
are the affections that make a woman and a man,
their household, and their homeland one.
These too, though known, cannot be told
to those who do not know them, and fewer
of us learn them, year by year.
These affections are leaving the world
like the colors of extinct birds,
like the songs of a dead language.

Think of the genius of the animals,
every one truly what it is:
gnat, fox, minnow, swallow, each made
of light and luminous within itself.
They know (better than we do) how
to live in the places where they live.
And so I would like to be a true
human being, dear reader—a choice
not altogether possible now.
But this is what I'm for, the side
I'm on. And this is what you should
expect of me, as I expect it of myself,
though for realization we may wait
a thousand or a million years.

And while I stood there
I saw more than I can tell
and I understood more than I saw,
for I was seeing in a sacred manner
the shapes of all things in the spirit
and the shape of all shapes as
they must all live together
as one being.

BLACK ELK

WINONA LADUKE, *activist and voice for Indigenous consciousness, has devoted her life to protecting the lands and lifeways of Native communities. Here she speaks of the importance of sacred sites, and how place belongs to our deeper understanding of spiritual ecology. She stresses the choices we need to make at this time.*

In the Time of the Sacred Places
WINONA LADUKE

*"It's not like a church where you have everything in one place.
We could describe how sacred sites are the teachers.... We don't
want the American dream.... We want our prayer rocks."*

—CALLEEN SISK, WINNEMUM WINTU

IN THE TIME OF Thunderbeings and Underwater
Serpents, the humans, animals, and plants conversed and
carried on lives of mischief, wonder, and mundane tasks.
The prophets told of times ahead, explained the causes of
the deluge of past, and predicted the two paths of the future:
one scorched and one green, one of which the Anishinaabeg
would have to choose.

In the time of the Thunderbeings and Underwater Serpents, it was understood that there was a constant balance
and a universe beyond this material world that needed to be
maintained and to whom we would belong always.

The Anishinaabe people, among other land-based
peoples, undulate between these worlds. The light of day,
the deepness of night remain; the parallel planes of spirit and
material world coexist in perpetuity. All remains despite the
jackhammer of industrial civilization, the sound of combus-
tion engines, and the sanitized white of a dioxin-bleached
day. That was then, but that is also now. Teachings, ancient
as the people who have lived on a land for five millennia,
speak of a set of relationships to all that is around, predicated
on respect, recognition of the interdependency of all beings,
an understanding of humans' absolute need to be reverent
and to manage our behavior, and an understanding that this

relationship must be reaffirmed through lifeways and through acknowledgment of the sacred.

Millennia have passed since that time, yet those beings still emerge: lightning strikes at unexpected times, the seemingly endless fires of climate change, tornadoes that flatten, King Tides, deluges of rivers, copper beings in the midst of industrial society. So it is that we come to face our smallness in a world of mystery, and our responsibilities to the life that surrounds us.

> We are a part of everything that is beneath us, above us and around us. Our past is our present, our present is our future, and our future is seven generations past and present.
>
> —HAUDENOSAUNEE TEACHING

In the midst of this time, land-based peoples work to continue such a lifeway, or to follow simply the original instructions passed on by Gichi Manidoo, the Creator, or those who instruct us. This path often is littered with the threats of a fossil-fuel and nuclear economy: a uranium mine, a big dam project, or the Tar Sands. People work to restore or retain their relationship to a sacred place and to a world. In many places, peoples hold Earth renewal ceremonies, for example, or water healing ceremonies. In an Indigenous philosophical view, these ceremonies are how we are able to continue. This essay tells some of those stories.

This essay also tells a story of a society based on the notion of frontier. Born of a doctrine of discovery, *terra nullius,* and a papal-driven entitlement to vanquish and destroy that which was Indigenous, America was framed in the mantra of Manifest Destiny. This settler-focused relationship to this North American continent has been historically one of conquest, of utilitarian relationship, of an anthropocentric taking of wealth to make more things for empire.

That society has named and claimed things: one mountain after another (Mt. Rainier, Harney Peak, Mt. McKinley, Mt. Lassen, Pikes Peak) all named, and claimed, for empire. *Naming and claiming with a flag does not mean relationship; it means only naming and claiming.* Americans have developed a sense of place related to empire, with no understanding that the Holy Land is also here. To name sacred mountain spirits after mortal men, who blow through for just a few decades, is to denude relationship.

Americans are also transient, taught an American dream of greener pastures elsewhere. This too belittles relationship to place. It holds no responsibility, only a sense of entitlement—to mineral rights, water rights, and private property—enshrined in the constitution.

In the times we find ourselves in, with the crashing of ecosystems, dying out of fish and trees, change and destabilization of climate, our relationship to place and to relatives—whether they have fins or roots—merits reconsideration.

ON SACRED PLACES

Since the beginning of times, the Creator and Mother Earth have given our peoples places to learn the teachings that will allow us to continue and reaffirm our responsibilities and ways on the lands from which we have come. Indigenous peoples are place-based societies, and at the center of those places are the most sacred of our sites, where we reaffirm our relationships.

Everywhere there are Indigenous people, there are sacred sites, there are ways of knowing, there are *relationships*. The people, the rivers, the mountains, the lakes, the animals, and the fish are all related. In recent years, US courts have challenged our ability to be in these places, and indeed to protect them. In many cases, we are asked to quantify "how sacred it is … or how often it is sacred."*Baffling concepts in the spiritual realm. Yet we do not relent, we are not capable of becoming subsumed.*

THE NUR & THE PEOPLE

In Northern California, the Winnemem Wintu have known since time immemorial of their relationships to the Nur, the salmon people. They have known that they have a sacred responsibility to protect and care for the salmon that have sustained them on the slope of Boyum Patuk, the sacred mountain, now known as Mt. Shasta. It was the Nur who gave the Winnemem their voice, who taught them to sing. The Winnemem were told long ago that if the salmon disappeared, so would they.

The salmon only sing as they course the rivers of the Northwest, and are only to be heard by the Wintu. Legends talk of a time when the Nur took pity on the Wintu people and gave to them their voice. The Wintu, in turn, were to care for the Nur always and were to sing. Millennia later they still try to fulfill this responsibility.

"The people believe that when the last salmon is gone, humans will be gone too," Caleen Sisk , traditional spiritual leader of the Winnemem Wintu, explains.

Millennia on the river did well for both the people and the salmon, in an area whose remoteness from white civilization was its protection. But in time that civilization encroached, and although they were signatories in good faith to what would be an unratified 1851 treaty, and later identified as the tribe who would be drowned in the 1941 federal act that created the Shasta Dam, the Winnemem Wintu ceased to exist as "Indians" under federal law. *This strange irony, that the government created by the settlers and intruders who took your land and killed your people gets to determine if you are still an Indian, remains particularly bitter to many tribes.* The Winnemem Wintu are particularly caught in this quagmire.

In 1941, the Shasta Dam drowned more than 26 miles of the lower McCloud River system, engulfing sacred sites, villages, and history under a deep lake destined to benefit cities far away, agriculture for the world, and tourists who could afford the way of life. The dam drowned much of the history of the Winnemem Wintu, and the dam blocked the passage of the salmon people—the McCloud River salmon. The Nur either interbred with the Sacramento River salmon, or died out in California.

Fish Rock was blown up to make room for a railroad track in 1914, which was, like so much else, drowned by the waters that would become known as Lake Shasta. What is left of Dekkas Rock, a prayer site, now protrudes from the reservoir, as one reporter notes, "… a malformed atoll." It was here, next to the river, that the Winnemem held what other tribes in the region call "Big Times," where disputes were adjudicated, songs and ceremonies were held, and marriages were arranged.

The Wintu grieved the loss of their salmon, and their sacred doctoring rocks, and the loss of the river, though their prophecies had foretold the loss of the salmon: "Our old people said that the salmon would be hidden behind a river of ice. Indian doctors and prophets had been with the Wintu long ago, and prophesied the time when the salmon would disappear," Caleen Sisk tells me.

That was almost unimaginable to the Wintu—or to those who "discovered the salmon" of the McCloud River. Livingston Stone, a fish culturist arriving in Wintu territory, noted that the spawning Chinook were so plentiful he could have walked across their backs from one side of the river to the other. In the 1870s, he established the Baird Hatchery on the McCloud, originally as an effort to breed a Pacific salmon to replenish the now dwindling and overfished Atlantic salmon stocks. The Winnemem Wintu, initially opposed to the fishery, made peace with the white men of the fisheries on the condition that the salmon would always be able to come home.

Then in a strange turning of events, in 1890, Livingston Stone decided to transplant the Wintu Nur to another world, Aotearoa, or New Zealand. Moved in sphagnum moss over a vast ocean, the Nur salmon people came to live in the Rakaia River on the South Island in Aotearoa (New Zealand).

So it was that the Nur, the salmon of the McCloud, disappeared from the Wintu world, but just as had been prophesied, they returned elsewhere, in a "river of ice"—the Rakaia River emerges from a glacial mountain. In 2008, the Wintu went to Aotearoa to visit their salmon. And, for the first time since the dams had destroyed their relatives, the Wintu sang once again for the Nur. It is fifty years since the dam destroyed the homeland of the salmon and much of the sacred world of the Wintu, but the Wintu believe that through prayer, prophecy, and hard work, there will be a return.

COPPER & IRON, WILD RICE & WATER, & WOLVES

> *"Sometimes it seems like people aren't interested in*
> *sticking around for another thousand years."*
> —MIKE WIGGINS, BAD RIVER ANISHINAABE
> TRIBAL CHAIRMAN

Two thousand miles to the East, on the shore of Gichi Gummi (Lake Superior), the Anishinaabeg Akiing ("the land to which the Anishinaabe people belong") stretches throughout the Great Lakes region in a territory of lakes and rivers, wild rice, and wolves.

On this land the Underwater Manidoowag, the Miskwaabik and Biwaabik spirits of copper and iron ore, have lived, *omaa akiing*, since the time of the Thunderbeings. As one early European explorer recorded, *"Copper was said to belong to the Underwater Manitouk.... One often finds at the bottom of the water, pieces of pure copper.... I have several times seen such pieces in the Savages' hand, and since they are superstitious, they keep to them as so many divinities, or as presents which the gods dwelling beneath the water have given them and on which their welfare is to depend."*

The Underwater Manidoowag, Miskwaabik and Biwaabik, were viewed not as spirits by the American government, but as objects of empire. Some of the first incursions by the US government onto Anishinaabeg land, in the early 1800s, were to secure access to iron and copper deposits. Within a very short period, four treaties were signed by the United States, each providing for mining in Anishinaabeg territory. By mid-century, more than 100 copper companies had been incorporated in the Anishinaabeg Akiing. Many of today's US-based transnational mining companies, including Kennecott, Anaconda Copper, and 3M, were founded in this era on the wealth of the Anishinaabeg.

The wild rice has also been here since the time of Thunderbeings. Indeed, it was a part of the Anishinaabeg migration story and of a set of prophecies instructing the people to *"go to the place where the food grows upon the water."* Called *manoomin* ("a seed of the Creator") by the Anishinaabe, wild rice is the only grain endemic to North America and is one of the greatest gifts imaginable to the land and waters. There are few other places in the world where such a bountiful gift is delivered to those who live there, whether they have wings or hands. Owing to the unique nature and adaptability of the *manoomin*, the lakes and rivers each year offer a wild rice crop at some place in the region. That is an amazing food security for a people and for the waterfowl who nest and eat in these same waters. It is because of this bounty that where there is wild rice there are Ojibwe or Anishinaabeg people, and where there are Anishinaabeg, there is wild rice. This is a sacred food and a keystone of the ecosystem of the Great Lakes region, or Anishinaabe Akiing. As copper and iron mining despoiled the waters of the lakes and rivers, so it devastated both the *manoomin* and those whose life and ways depended upon it.

The decimation of the Anishinaabeg by plagues, starvation, and federal policies closely mirrored the destruction of the *ma'iingan*, the wolf. The Anishinaabeg relationship to the *ma'iingan* is deeply sacred in the traditions and history of the people. It is said that the first friend of the half spirit/half human being Naanaaboozhoo, a central figure in Anishinaabeg culture and teachings, was the *ma'iingan*. In Anishinaabeg prophecies, *that which befalls the wolf will befall the Anishinaabeg*. The limiting of territories—to reservations for the Anishinaabeg and to a few refuges and a few sparse patches of the north woods for the wolves—occurred for both. Like the people, the wolves were brought to near-extinction.

Yet both wolves and Anishinaabeg have returned to the northland. Today, nineteen Anishinaabeg reservations span the north country, from Michigan into Montana. This same territory is today the home of the largest wolf population in the lower forty-eight states. Where there are 60,000 Anishinaabeg, there are 5,000 wolves—both relatives, one with two legs and one with four, rebounding after catastrophic losses.

THE PREDATOR RETURNS

The companies forged of empire in the 1850s are also returning home now, having ravaged the world, fortified their empires, and left memorials to the copper that once was, in the form of huge pits. New mines are proposed throughout the Anishinaabe Akiing. Thus far they have been fended off by citizens and tribal opposition, but the region is incredibly challenged, as Ojibwes note in a letter to the United Nations requesting assistance: *"Currently, an aggressive mining boom throughout Anishinaabeg territory, of present-day Michigan, Wisconsin, Minnesota, and Ontario, threatens the water quality and ecosystem of almost every sub-watershed of Lake Superior."*

Eagle Rock, known as "the Home of the White Wolf," is a sacred site and prehistoric navigation site on the Keewenaw. It is considered sacred to not only the Anishinaabeg, but also the Hochunk and Cheyenne peoples. The tribes living today in this territory, as well as the National Congress of American Indians, have requested that the rock be protected as a site of religious worship.

Underneath the rock, in a world below, is Miskwaabik Aabinoojiins, or the Copper Child. This copper ore body, appearing in GIS imaging as a baby, awaits its scheduled end like a convict on death row: Rio Tinto Zinc, a UK-based mining company, through its subsidiary Kennecott, plans to mine the copper deposit adjacent to the sacred place.

It has been a seven-year battle for the sacred site, marked by arrests and legal actions, and now by a petition to the United Nations for intervention under the *Declaration on the Rights of Indigenous Peoples* not only to protect their sacred sites, but to be protected from minerals exploitation, which will destroy the aquatic ecosystems of wild rice and a rich land upon which the Anishinaabeg have lived for five millennia.

The Michigan regulatory authorities, which have taken jurisdiction over the area, have ruled against the tribes, the water, and the sacred site, stating essentially that the site could not be sacred or did not have spiritual significance because a place of worship must be a building. On these grounds, the state approved the mining permit.

Proposals in both Wisconsin and Minnesota would eviscerate water quality laws, with severe impacts on the wild rice or *manoomin* of the north. In turn, the recent delisting of the wolf by the US Fish and Wildlife seems synchronized exactly with the interests of new mining companies in the region.

But it is a time when relationships are changing. It is ironic that the two largest challenges to the wholesale mining of the north may be *manoomin*, or wild rice, and the *ma'iingan*. Tribal communities, joined increasingly by northern residents, have opposed the threats to water and wild rice throughout the north country, and regulatory battles are underway in Minnesota. And, while the wolf has been delisted by federal agencies under the Endangered Species Act, tribal communities are opposing the delisting in their territories. This is significant, as the wolf territories coincide with reservations and the areas surrounding tribal reservations still within tribal jurisdiction due to treaties and court decisions.

In this time, tribal governments and intergovernment agencies in the north pledge to retain their relationship and responsibility to the *ma'iingan*, and our communities remain vigilant in working to protect the sacred beings from the mines of the predator.

DOKO'OO'SLIID ... THE MOUNTAIN OF KACHINAS & RECYCLED SKI AREAS

To the far south, in the realm of the sacred mountains of the Dine or Navajo people, Dine Bii Kaya, the four sacred mountains, are again facing threats. Mt. Taylor is once again proposed for uranium mining, and Doko'oo'sliid, the Sacred Mountain of the West to the Navajo, is being desecrated for the pleasure of skiers.

This volcanic highland area of Arizona began forming over 6 million years ago with the eruption of nearly 600 volcanoes. The most dramatic of those eruptions created a place sacred to thirteen tribes, a cluster of three 12,000-foot mountain peaks known as the Sacred Mountain of the West, one of four cornerstones marking the borders of Dine Bii

Kaya, the land of the Dine or Navajo. The Dine know it as a place where the Kachina spirits emerge. In the proud vernacular of American empire, the sacred mountain is called San Francisco Peaks.

The highest point in Arizona, the only arctic-alpine vegetation in the state, which grows here in a fragile two-square-mile zone, and Arizona's best examples of Ice Age glaciation all can be found here. It has been a place for the gathering of sacred herbs and the practice of religious ceremonies since the dawn of time.

In 1984, the United States Congress recognized the fragile ecosystems and cultural significance of the area and designated the Kachina Peaks Wilderness. Yet here, in this unlikely place, in an ostensibly protected Wilderness in the desert, a ski resort has been proposed, with a plan to pipe treated sewage water from Flagstaff to spray artificial snow on the sacred mountain. There is no water source on the mountain other than what falls from the sky.

Despite the known ecosystem, archeological and cultural issues, and determined opposition from Native nations and conservation organizations, the Ninth US Circuit Court of Appeals recently allowed the Arizona Snowbowl Recreation project to proceed with its plan. Flagstaff-treated sewer water will be trucked to Snowbowl until a 14.8-mile pipeline is complete, and then some 180 million gallons a year of treated effluent from the city of Flagstaff will be pumped up the sacred mountain to the ski area for snowmaking. The treated sewage has been proven to contain contaminants such as pharmaceuticals and hormones. Snowbowl hopes to attract ski-starved desert dwellers to its resort with clever marketing, but it remains to be seen how enticing a mouthful of Snowbowl effluent cocktail might be.

The Snowbowl owners have already clear-cut some 74 acres of rare alpine forest for new ski runs. A 10-million-gallon retention pond and another 12 miles of pipeline will be built to distribute reclaimed sewer water along the ski runs, all desecrations in the eyes of the Dine people. In the summer of 2012, protests continued in defense of a sacred place, in a call for access to water for people and the land, and ultimately in a questioning of priorities.

This is the difference between worldviews, one that views a land as a rich ore body, or a playground, and another that views it as a source of great spiritual and cultural wealth…. This is the story of the time in which we find ourselves.

THE AUCTION OF THE SACRED

As the wind breathes out of Wind Cave, I am reminded of the creation of humans and my own small place in this magnificent world. Wind Cave National Park in the Black Hills is named for the cave itself, called *Washun Niya*, ("the Breathing Hole of Mother Earth") by the Lakota People. In the Lakota creation story, it is from here that they emerged to this world.

It is a complex cave system. According to scientists, we may only have a sense of five percent of the cave's volume and breadth, and likely even less of its power. Some might call this the *"known unknown."* Most Indigenous peoples would understand it as *the Great Mystery*—that which is much larger than our own anthropocentric understanding of the world—reflecting the understanding that, indeed, there is more than one world surrounding people.

So it is that in 2012, a time of change and transformation signaled in an American election year and predicted in the Mayan Calendar, we find the smallness and the greatness of humans in the much larger world around us coming face-to-face in the Black Hills. A most sacred place, *Pe'Sla*, in the center of the Lakota Universe, came up for sale, and values and worldviews clashed.

Pe'Sla, to the Lakota, is "Center of the Heart of Everything that is ... one of a small number of highly revered and geographically-cosmologically integral places on the entire planet," according to Lakota scholar Chase Iron Eyes. It is "the place where Morning Star, manifested as a meteor, fell to earth to help the Lakota by killing a great bird that had taken the lives of seven women; Morning Star's descent having created the wide open uncharacteristic bald spot in the middle of the forested Black Hills. (On American maps, this is called Old Baldy.) The Morning Star placed the spirits of those seven women in the sky as the constellation 'Pleiades' or 'The Seven Sisters.'"

On August 25, 2012, the Center of the Heart of Everything was to be placed on the auction block, destined to be diced into a set of 300-acre tracts proposed for ranchettes, with a possible road through the heart of what has been, until now, a relatively un-desecrated sacred site. "We didn't even know it was going to be sold," Debra White Plume from Manderson told me. "We heard nothing about it until we saw the auction announcement."

America is a country where private property is enshrined as a constitutional right, but the rights of nature, of the natural world, or of unborn generations are not. In the time of the crashing of ecosystems and worlds, it may be worth not making a commodity out of all that is revered. A 2005 editorial in the generally very conservative Rapid City Journal points out that protecting Lakota sacred sites is of interest to all. *"Non-Indians have little to fear if familiar sites are designated as sacred; visitors are still allowed at Bear Butte, Devil's Tower, and Rainbow Bridge, even though they are being managed as Indian sacred sites. And in fact, expanding non-Indians' knowledge and appreciation of the Indian lore surrounding such sites could lead to greater cultural understanding."*

With less than two weeks remaining before *Pe'Sla* was to be auctioned off, word spread through Lakota communities (three of which, all Lakota reservations, are in the economically poorest counties in the country), through the use of Facebook, the Internet, and the media, from the *Huffington Post* to the *Seattle Times*. The story of the Lakota people, their sacred site, and the proposed auction was repeated in whispers, and then in rallies and in outrage. Using the Internet, the communities raised over half a million dollars, which was then matched by tribal money originating with the Rosebud Sioux Tribe, and other donations. The auction was cancelled, and the Lakota people have begun to negotiate for the purchase of their sacred site.

It is incredibly ironic, however, in many ways, particularly considering that the *Paha Sapa*, the Black Hills, was never purchased from the Lakota but illegally taken by the United States with the advent of gold mining (the Hearst empire). Though over $105 million was allocated for the Black Hills by Congress to pay Lakota people for the illegal taking, that money has never been accepted. Hence the irony: the people must buy back land they have never considered owned by anyone else.

ON A RETURN TO SACRED LIFEWAYS

There is always hope, and for those of us who remain involved in our ceremonies, there is also faith. That faith is reaffirmed when small miracles of spirit occur, and the world changes.

On the banks of the McCloud River in Northern California, the Wintu gather, despite citations and legal opposition by the state of California, to hold their sacred coming-of-age ceremonies for their young women. This is how life continues.

And, one day, not too far away, those salmon will return home from Aotearoa. And there will be a celebration of the Nur and the Wintu.

In the northwoods, the Anishinaabeg celebrate one round of opposing the Beast. In 2012, the huge GTAC mine in the Penokee Mountains of Wisconsin—the headwaters to the Bad River, the centerpiece of the Bad River tribal community of Anishinaabeg—was defeated, like another four before it in Wisconsin. The defeat may be temporary, but it is breathing room for Mother Earth.

And in 2012, it seems that *Pe'Sla* will be protected from becoming a set of luxury ranchettes, and may continue as a place where a people pray and reaffirm their relationship to Creation.

And then there is the renaming, or the recovery of names. Several decades ago, Mt. McKinley became Mt. Denali. On the other side of the world, Australia's Ayers Rock became Uluru, in the name of the people who live there, not the white man who found it. In 2010, in Canada, the Haida homeland was formally renamed Haida Gwaii, eclipsing Queen Charlotte Island, named for a Queen who had likely never seen that land nor understood Haida traditions. And further south, the Salish Sea is emerging in what was Puget Sound, and more reaffirmations of place and history are reframing our understanding of the holy land that is here. These stories join with the stories of a people and their allies who have come to live on this land.

On a larger scale, the New Zealand Courts have recently affirmed the rights of a River to exist, in a court system that emerged from colonial and church authorities. The Whanganui River became a legal entity under the name Te Awa Tupua ("an integrated, living whole") and was given the same status as a person under New Zealand law in 2012.

The industrial predator, however, is unrelenting. Voracious in appetite, greed, and lacking any heart, all that is becomes prey ...

If 57 percent of the energy produced in the US is wasted through inefficiencies, one might want to become less wasteful to survive. And if two-thirds of our material-based economy ends up in waste dumps relatively quickly, we may want to cut our consumption. These are economic choices, political choices, and personal choices. And they ultimately have to do with empire, the need for new frontiers, and making peace, *omaa akiing*, here on this land.

In the din of crashing worlds, it is possible to watch and breathe. In the 2012 deluge of the city of Duluth, rain fell constantly for two days onto the streets of a city with aging infrastructure. The Anishinaabeg remember a great flood from the earliest of memories, after which the world was made anew. The Anishinaabeg watched the flood from our reservations, an island safely away from this deluge and crash.

The tally in economic terms of the 2012 flood is somewhere around $100 million. That figure represents just the beginning of climate-change-related expenses in this year. By March of 2012, there had been over 129,000 recorded weather records on a worldwide scale. World insurance agencies project that we will be spending 20 percent of our GDP on a worldwide scale on climate-change-related disasters.

The polar bear is freed by the Duluth deluge from the zoo, escaping his pen. As the bear headed north from the Duluth Zoo, we Anishinaabeg knew that the time was changing. We watched and we understood that we, as sacred beings in this millennium, have an opportunity to do a righteous and *pono* thing—to take a good path.

In the time of Thunderbeings and Underwater Serpents, the humans, animals, and plants conversed and carried on lives of mischief, wonder, and mundane tasks. The prophets told of times ahead, explained the deluge of past and predicted the two paths of the future: one scorched and one green, one of which the Anishinaabeg would have to choose.

All of us have the same choice, and somewhere in this time, there is the potential to take a right path.

*The old Lakota was wise. He knew that man's heart
away from nature becomes hard; he knew that lack of
respect for growing, living things soon led to
lack of respect for humans too.*

CHIEF LUTHER STANDING BEAR

Scientist, philosopher, feminist, author, environmentalist, and activist VANDANA SHIVA *is a one-woman movement for peace, sustainability, and social justice. In 1991 she founded Navdanya, a national movement to protect the diversity and integrity of living resources, especially native seeds. Here she speaks of how food connects us to the web of life, and calls us to remember that* annadana, *the gift and giving of food, is sacred.*

Annadana: The Gift of Food
Vandana Shiva

THE FOOD WE EAT, the food that nourishes us, is a gift from the earth, from the sun, from millions of years of evolution.

It is also a gift from the farmers, livestock herders, fisher folk, who till the land, care for animals, and harvest fish. When we forget the earth from where we receive our food, food becomes non-sustainable. Food is life. Food is not just our vital need: it is the web of life.

As the *Taittiriya Upanishad* says:

> From food (*anna*), verily, creatures are produced
> Whatsoever (creatures) dwell on the earth....
> For truly, food is the chief of beings [1]

> Beings here are born from food, when born
>   they live by food,
> On deceasing they enter into food. [2]

Food is alive: it is not just pieces of carbohydrate, protein, and nutrient, it is a being; it is a sacred being.

> Verily, they obtain all food
> Who worship Brahma as food. [3]

In the words of *Maha Ashwamedhika*:

> The giver of the food is the giver of life,
>   and indeed of everything else,
> Therefore, one who desires well-being in
>   this world and beyond should
> Specially endeavour to give food....
> Food is indeed the preserver of life
>   and food is the source of procreation.[4]

Because food is the very basis of creation, food is creation, and it is the Creator. It is Divinity in the context of the way we live: there are all kinds of duties that we should be performing with respect to it.

If people have food it is because society has not forgotten those duties. If people are going hungry, society has moved away from the ethical duties related to food.

Annadana is the gift and giving of food. All other ethical arrangements in society get looked after if everyone is engaging in *annadana* on a daily basis. According to an ancient Indian saying: "There is no *dana* greater than *annadana* and *tirthadana*—the giving of food to the hungry and water to the thirsty."

Or, again, in the words of the *Taittiriya Brahmana*:

> Do not send away anyone who comes to your door
> without offering him food and hospitality.
>
> This is the inviolable discipline of humankind:
> therefore have a great abundance of food and exert
> all your efforts towards ensuring such abundance,
> and announce to the world that this abundance of
> food is ready to be partaken by all.

Thus from the culture of giving you have the conditions of abundance, and the sharing by all.

In another scripture it is said:

I forsake the one that eats without giving,
I am the *annadevtaa* (the god of food, the divine
    in food);
I come and go according to my own discipline,
I nurture the one for whom giving carries the
    same significance as eating,
To him I reach in plenty: I remain out of reach of
    the other who eats without giving,
Who amongst men can deter me, the *annadevtaa*,
    from my course?

When we forget our *Annadatas*, the food producers, we create hunger and poverty. An agriculture without people becomes an agriculture dominated by agribusiness, by fossil fuels, by agrichemicals and poisons.

There is a predominant myth that industrial corporate agriculture produces more food. This is what justifies destruction of small farms and small farmers. However, this false productivity only measures commodities per labour input, not food and nutrition per unit land or water or energy. On the one hand this hides the high output of small, biodiverse, organic farms. On the other hand it hides the high external input of industrial monocultures, which use ten times more energy than they produce as food. Industrial farms also use ten times more water than ecological farms.

As a result, nutrition disappears from our farms along with the farmers. And the environment is burdened with toxics and greenhouse gases. Climate Change, erosion of biodiversity, depletion and pollution of water are the consequence. If these costs were internalized, we could not afford to eat poisoned foods.

Medicine and sickness heal each other.
The whole world is medicine.
Where do you find yourself?

ZEN MASTER YUNMEN,
NINTH-CENTURY CHINA

SUSAN MURPHY ROSHI *is a Zen teacher who offers a unique spiritual perspective in seeing our ecological crisis as "a tremendous koan set for us by the Earth, speaking to us plainly in words we cannot yet fully understand." To answer this living koan, we "need to relearn the fundamentals that were once natural to us."*

The Koan of the Earth
Susan Murphy

You cannot solve a problem
with the thinking that created it.
—ATTRIBUTED TO ALBERT EINSTEIN

"EARTH IS WHERE we all live. Earth sustains us. Earth allows us to be here temporarily. Like a good guest, we respect our host and all the beauty and bounty we are lucky to experience. We do no harm. And then we leave." This comment was posted as part of a website discussion, and it's pretty hard to argue with it, actually.

However, our industrialized world constructs itself in reverse image to inarguable reality. We live walled off from the earth as far as possible, though we will pay a high price for views of water or mountains. Many of us would by now find it unnatural to lie down to sleep on the earth, gather and cook food where we are, drink water from a creek, defecate in a hole dug in the ground. Our air-conditioned, plugged-in level of material comfort estranges us from the earth and even from the sense of what is natural. And it insulates us from the high cost of this intensely self-centered way of living, leaving that to be borne out of sight by other people, other species, the earth as a whole. We live at maximum distance from the fact that we are here only temporarily, that we will age and die. Not only do we not respect our host and acknowledge the bounty and beauty earth pours out for us, we comprehensively distract ourselves from that by any means available. If pushed to notice it, we reassure ourselves that the mounting tsunami of harm left in our wake is entirely unintentional, not under our control.

"Doing no harm" to the earth remains low on the agenda of an intensely industrialized, energy-hungry world. Seven billion of us are now transfixed by an impossible promise of all securing the extreme material and technological advantages presently lavished upon members of the industrialized world. The dense forms of energy—harnessed first from coal and then so spectacularly from oil—have lifted the material lives of a growing number of us to levels of physical ease undreamed of in earlier generations, and this has happened so rapidly it has been hard to catch up with all the harsh implications—though they are certainly now catching up on us.

If human beings ever were "entitled" to make such short-term expendable use of the earth, it follows that all are equally entitled to the carbon-fuelled dream of unending bounty once enjoyed only by the West. The paradigm of continual economic growth insists that this is realizable and good, and in fact that all of human well-being depends upon indefinite expansion of the market.

The problem is that the price of this indefinite expansion turns out to be the forfeiture of climatic conditions hospitable to our species. And of course not only to *our* species. The great extinction spasm we are living through right now, which could well include us, is tearing down the intricately interlaced ecologies of the earth as mere collateral damage in the pursuit of a single-minded, self-entitled idea. Too bad that it is extinguishing all "entitlement" to life forever for hundreds of earth's life forms every single day—while we continue to add more than 220 new human lives to the planet every second, or more than 200,000 every day.

From a position of accustomed comfort it is hard to conceive of living in a way that would require greater personal skill, effort, and care to manifest the necessities of life. Breaking our reliance on the oil that has shown signs of peaking and beginning an inexorable decline, at exactly the time it has become woven into every detail of our lifestyle, is seemingly impossible to contemplate. Yet any child can see through the magical thinking and selfishness that underpin the economic imperatives of limitless material growth and mindless waste—that nevertheless will duly go on to shape their adult lives.

The dream of an infinitely expandable planet placed entirely at our disposal was always just that, a dream, and it's fast becoming a nightmare. Tumultuous change on a vast scale grows increasingly likely with every day of business as usual. The only question is what forms it will take, which order of climate shocks and political crises will start to shake our world apart, and how people will react as the market collapses and the source of plenty evaporates.

THE MAGIC FLOW OF PLENTY

An old Scottish fairy tale told of a fortunate village to which the fairies had given a magic cask in return for some good turn. Any time there was something to celebrate, the villagers just turned the tiny spigot and the wine and communal goodwill would flow, inexhaustible. Everything went along beautifully until the day a curious housemaid decided to see just exactly how it all worked. She unscrewed the tiny spigot and took a peek inside. Nothing there but dust and ancient spiderwebs. And from that time on, the fairy wine cask yielded not a single drop of magic wine.

There are many ways to read this story in the light of our time. One is that we must never look too closely at what produces the magic flow of plenty we dream will continue forever. Look inside at its dark workings and the happy dream of "forever" will be shattered. Scarcity, dust, and ruin are waiting to be discovered inside it.

Another is that the earth sustains our life with its magical weave of infinite relationships of mutual dependency between all life forms and the elements that sustain them— water, air, soil, minerals, sunlight…. Some call this peerless magic "ecology," or "nature." Others may see it as the grace that animates creation. Failing to trust and protect this perpetually self-renewing gift, attempting instead to exploit it as a bounty earmarked for our exclusive use, we tear the web of life apart.

Let's take a kind of quick housemaid's peek inside the industrialized version of the fairy barrel and trace the biography of a typical North American tomato, as Peter Bahouth has described it. A genetically patented hybrid tomato derived from a Mexican strain is grown on land originally farmed by Mexican farmers in agricultural cooperatives. The new strain has low tolerance for local conditions, so the land is fumigated with an intensely ozone-depleting chemical, methyl bromide, then doused in pesticides. The toxic waste from production of these chemicals is shipped to one of the world's largest chemical dumps in Alabama, which is situated in a poor black neighborhood, with marked effects on local health. The Mexican farmworkers, displaced from their cooperatives but permitted to apply the pesticide to the plants now grown on what was once their farmland, are given no protection or instructions in proper application of such dangerous substances. They are paid around $2.50 a day and offered no form of health care.

The tomatoes are placed on plastic-foam trays and covered in plastic wrap, then packed in cardboard boxes. The plastic wrap is manufactured in Texas, where local residents suffer exposure to the dioxins that are by-products of chlorine manufacture and highly hazardous to their health. The cardboard boxes, which were once three-hundred-year-old trees harvested from an old-growth forest in British Columbia, are manufactured thousands of miles distant in the Great Lakes district, then shipped by truck all the way back to Latin American farms, using oil extracted and processed in Mexico.

The boxed tomatoes are artificially ripened with ether. Now watery, weary, and nutritionally compromised, the tomatoes are sent by refrigerated trucks on vast freeway networks all over North America. Ozone-depleting CFC cooling equipment is used at every stage of their delivery to the tables of "consumers" (once called "people"), who are bound to wonder what on earth has happened to that delectable fruit that once went by the name "tomato."

While there is no evil master plan of ecological destruction in this story, and little *conscious* intent to destroy communities and lifeways, disfigure the countryside, and ruin the climate, nevertheless it is one small part of an overarching system that effectively does evil by way of countless repetitive, cumulative failures of care and conscience, easily brushed aside in the process of maximizing profit.

Nature always was and still is the real magic barrel. Its gift economy of ever-evolving life provided the original soil, water, seed, and flowering plants, and eventually the small green fruit that could be coaxed by human ingenuity and toil into large, juicy tomatoes. The industrial super-magic barrel took over from there, turning this cyclical flow of gifts into a one-way flow of profit into a few hands. The product was wrought from nature at extraordinary cost to natural systems, while its engineers refuse point-blank to register on its balance sheets the vast destruction of "natural capital" that it involves. That's a "magic" that fast wears out its welcome.

Incidentally, there's no report in the story of the fairy-barrel village ever sharing its great luck with any neighboring villages. The village apparently felt secure in its superior fortune, and a sense of entitlement no doubt helped cover over its naked mean-spiritedness. But a fairy gift can be double-edged. Misuse exceptional good fortune and you become cold and alienated, poverty-stricken in ways you may not even notice. Until the next time you try to turn the tiny magic spigot and find the supply of all that really matters most has run out forever.

MIND AND WORLDS

These days I can find myself in many worlds—or at least entertaining many propositions about what this world is and what its fate may be—in even a single day. A whole flicker of darting thought and retreat from thought, like schools of fish, surging this way then that. News of gigantic Antarctic ice shelves breaking away; the Gulf of Mexico fast becoming a vast ocean dead spot; the Great Barrier Reef expected not to survive beyond two more decades; phytoplankton, the foundation of the entire marine food chain, reduced by 40 percent since 1950 due to warming seawater; island nations pleading eloquently and uselessly in Copenhagen and Cancun; global poverty set to skyrocket with climate collapse; the gap between rich and poor growing to obscene extreme.... My thoughts dart this way and that, surging like schools of fish, and my emotions follow. In the never-ending avalanche of factoids, opinions, gossip, trivia, brands, and sound bites, there is no space or sufficient quiet for sorrow, reflection, and resolve.

Is it like this for you? How are you dealing with it?

When I walk out into the world, well away from phones, i-gadgets, Internet, radio, television, or newsprint, and walk on the earth and breathe the open air, I begin to recollect my-self and come back to earth. I gradually become a humble, humorous, earthy human being again, who belongs here as thoroughly as every natural thing I can find around me. This may be easier in the green and flowing world that lies beyond the nearly perfect human trance we call a city, but even in the city the earth is always in reach; and when the earth is in reach, wonder is in spitting distance. The weed-life taking root in the cracks of the pavement, a glimpse of a pelican moving above the buildings, a cat's cool stare from a warm brick wall, a puddle riffled by breeze disturbing its upside-down reflections, a tree root powering its slow way out of the asphalt and into a gutter....

Just as they draw my attention, my attention calls them back to vivid life. Consciousness is partner to the compos-ing of a "world." Every sentient being creates an entire world according to its earth-given style of sentience and its experience of life. The world of the blowfly blundering into a room will be utterly unlike the world of the person trying to ignore its frantic buzzing, though both breathe the same air and drink the same water. The poet Anne Carson says, "There is no person without a world"; equally, there is no "world," in the fully human, conscious sense of that word, without a person. Every human death takes with it an entire and unrepeatable world, a whole realm of memories, dreams, reflections, beliefs, and observations. We suffer this fact in the loss of each other, and in fear of our own imagined loss of ourselves. If we do finally swat that blundering blowfly with a tea towel, what can we really know of the world ex-tinguished in a single swipe?

Although there are countless trillions of worlds alive on earth, in 1968 astronauts Lovell, Anders, and Borman of the Apollo 8 space mission became the first beings to leave earth's orbit and see our one entire blue-green planet swim-ming in black space. The depth of surprise and awe in those three men suggests they witnessed not merely an amazing physical fact but a surpassing and singular miracle. They found themselves deeply stirred by this planet's luminous presence. Earth brought them to tears.

Until we can expand our scope beyond self-centered and purely human concerns to hold in mind the trillion worlds alive on this one earth at any moment, and to glimpse *ourselves* exactly in that vibrant, seamless web of interconnectedness, we are living in a kind of madness—which is to say, not living in reality. The great question of our time is whether or not we will prove able to wake into full awareness of the earth, and the geophysical changes now in play, in time to avert full-blown catastrophe.

Even beyond skillful crisis management and regaining the intelligence needed for survival, such a challenge actually offers the exhilarating chance to reawaken to our real nature, which has never departed one inch from reality. For what is realization or enlightenment but the earth speaking to us directly, with our own noise no longer overwhelming the signal?

The unending call and response between human mind and Planet Earth can be dimmed but it cannot be turned off. It can be hard to hear over the avalanche of distractions, but the moment our resistance softens or just mysteriously gives way, it cannot be silenced. At that moment we have arrived at the place where truly *minding* the earth begins.

Our increasing impertinence (to use a word which originally meant not just rudeness but lack of relevance) is that we have, somewhere in the march of "civilization," lost the humble amazement of feeling the earth and ourselves to be a prodigious unearned gift from the universe. How did we make ourselves self-appointed lords of the earth and, like spoilt children, throw all gratitude and humility out the window?

A deeper chord of human-earth relatedness composes the very cells of our body and lies entirely undisturbed by all our puerile strutting; but while we cannot kill the fundamental relatedness, we have broken our accord with the earth, and that may have us ejected yet again from Eden—this time setting fire to the Ark on the way.

"The world," from our earliest emergence as a species, has always signified a human project entwined completely with nature. But the advent of human agency in shaping the earth has now reached a point where the fate of much of the biosphere of the planet is in the slippery, forgetful hands of human beings. And we have forgotten that our fate, too, is completely entwined with the fate of the earth.

FACING THE MUSIC

When the full scope of the damage we live by is fully taken in, it is undeniably crushing. I think we've all felt a terrible sense of being frozen in the headlights of an unstoppable juggernaut. That juggernaut is the globalized coal- and oil-based military-industrial-media economy, along with its vast web of national corporate power relations, digital information, opinions, and gossip. It is greased equally by foreign wars and the seamless collusion of all who enjoy the comfortable living conditions and infinite distractions of the industrially developed countries of the world. All of us on board the juggernaut have chosen to live obliviously towards its immense destruction of the earth's natural capital. We have deregulated ferociously unrestrained corporate entities, licensing them to exploit the earth's "resources" without mercy, just as if they were limitless.

It is an unlovely and fearful sight.

And yet, have a look: the juggernaut is not separate from us. We are staring with growing fear and disgust at something that is not "safely" outside ourselves but exists with our own full-blown participation. Cursing the drug dealer does not free us from being junkies. With the exception of those living entirely off the grid in every respect, by necessity or choice, there is not a man, woman, or child in the industrialized world who does not lend themselves daily in some measure to the all-consuming appetite that is exhausting the earth's resources.

Wherever the juggernaut arrives, it devours rivers, mountains, forests, oceans, peoples, creatures, and every sign of the loveliness, benevolence, and balance of the natural world, leaving nothing indigenous, wise, beautiful, various, or whole in the debris of its wake. Just a flat, homogenized streak of so-called civilization: strip malls, car parks, industrial "parks," concrete, smog, and endless high-rise. Or in a poor country, not even that—just black plastic bags in the wind, intensified poverty, and rampant exploitation of people and natural resources. The juggernaut we all help create—by failing to resist its stream of "things" and "stuff," by turning a blind eye to its evils, by fearing it when it shows itself to be beyond moderating—is not driven by malevolence. It is powered by the usual array of human vices, but magnified exponentially by the speed and reach offered by oil and digitalized communication.

The juggernaut pushes a barbarous worldview that has, in the last three decades, gradually left all public forms of caretaking and altruism—towards each other and all life on earth—almost entirely to voluntarism and religion. It is a worldview that still understands "we" and "us" in national and sporting terms, but barely at all in societal terms.

I think we are all aware by now that the emperor of limitless consumption and economic growth has no shred of morality to cover the nakedness of its greed. But I think we also know that with the naming and exposure of the emperor, there goes "the lifestyle."

Is this why the moment that global warming began to make a strong moral, physical, and practical claim on our attention, a blizzard of blinding denial was immediately unleashed? Public relations skills, honed on seeding doubt about the effects of Big Tobacco on public health, have been applied to a campaign aimed at seeding climate-change denial under the rubric of "skepticism"—a handsomely funded snow job traceable back to Big Oil. At the same time, all moves to decarbonize the economy have been branded a plot to destroy jobs and ruin the nation, despite the fact that a more comprehensive destroyer of jobs and nations than climate and environmental collapse is impossible to imagine.

We must find a livable transition away from an economic system that is at war with the earth, but weighing up the harms between different courses of action and inaction will be extremely challenging. Yet if we manage to accept the challenge, the intense rigor of responding to this great question of our time can wake up forgotten parts of ourselves and usher in our maturity as a species. The shared peril of global warming is not just an economic and political matter but an overwhelming "moral opportunity," as Al Gore has called it, to restore effective ethical brakes to a worldview religiously devoted to rapacious self-interest.

My tone of hope is tempered by awareness of the grossly unequal material conditions of humanity—a gap in justice and sanity that has grown astronomically in the last fifty years, and promises to yawn ever more widely as climate change impacts water and food security in the developing world (as we fondly call it from our padded sofas). I reflect on our shared emergency from a relatively easy first-world life; without that luxury, my chance to do so would be severely curtailed. I am also aware of how easily our comfort can insulate us for just a little bit longer from the sharp end of the emergency of climate change and global poverty already being endured by a majority of people on earth.

Any illusion that we can safely enjoy the present flow of costly abundance is its own catastrophe ahead of the train wreck. To the extent that we find it possible to delay responding and defer paying attention, we are suffering diminished ability to think and move in timely reaction to danger. Our equivocation and easy distractibility is a form of succumbing in advance to the disaster. It enables our present limp state of political leadership, permits the shameful discrediting of those who publish hard scientific findings, and retards the push towards a shared, cogent vision of the magnitude of change that must come.

How did we let ourselves fall so deeply asleep at the wheel?

The neoliberal economic "rationalism" to which the global economy has been wedded for the past three decades has almost completely disengaged a political "we" who can respond to serious threat. Margaret Thatcher's infamous "there is no society, there are only individuals" has burgeoned into the extreme egotism of a materially driven individualism and left us no longer very able to build solidarity around a coherent political position. For decades we have seemed unable to believe in or even perceive a threat that so directly addresses something called "us all"; any threat that was not "all about me" appeared to be undetectable.

Planetary crisis has so far been addressed purely in terms of "the thinking that created the problem." Take the longest and richest coral reef system on the planet that stretches for more than a thousand miles just off the coast of Queensland. In 2007, signs of coral bleaching in the Great Barrier Reef became impossible to ignore. It seems hard to believe now, but the then Prime Minister of Australia, John Howard, suggested that this could be "solved" by simply erecting shade structures over the most tourist-accessible sections of the reef.

Such "problem solving" glides serenely past the stark fact that, besides being one of the most prolific sites of biodiversity on the planet, the reef is a *whole*—a most intricately and delicately balanced ecology of fish, crustacean, shell, and coral species—not a series of "spots." And that likewise the warming of seawater that is killing the reef is part of a *whole* ocean system of currents. Most of all, it entirely disavows the fact that the reef is being killed by a global economic system that can never afford to admit to the fundamental flaw of its logic of limitless expansion on a finite planet. As for the possibility of seeing that the highly heat-stressed state of the largest coral reef on earth beginning to suffer a degradation of its complexity that threatens its entire collapse presents something much deeper than a problem to be solved, that it poses a profoundly important moral and metaphysical question to every human being alive today—this does not even begin to dawn at the horizon of such severely compromised thinking.

AN INESCAPABLE OPPORTUNITY

We are living in what must surely be the most daunting and arresting moment we have ever faced as a species. We face a developing reality that can either condemn human beings to oblivion or inspire us to wake up to our lives in a dramatically more interesting way. A way that begins in living soberly and creatively towards the crisis of our planet—not as a problem to be solved by engineering an ever better, safer human "bubble," but as a constantly unfolding obligation to begin considering the remaking of ourselves as ecologically awake human beings.

It is possible to live straight on to our reality instead of hiding out from it in ten thousand different ways. To do so, first we have to see through the way our sense of the world has been framed by the stories that form the bedrock of our civilization, stories that pose nature as a dubious force to be mastered and utilized, or put more bluntly, raped and pillaged for profit.

To the extent that these stories no longer explain the many things that urgently need explaining, they have become untrue. We can no longer adhere to "truths" that we have depended on to steer civilization in a trustworthy direction. At the same time, we have to recognize the need for a common story that can help us understand and engage with the new reality breaking upon our heads.

In the stories we tell, as one Kwakiutl elder said, we tell *ourselves*. What would we find ourselves to be, and how would we behave, if we were to live with all of our human ingenuity brought to bear upon living within the terms of the earth instead of despite them? If we were to recognize the rights of earth and other species in law, to mould agricultural and economic choices and the design of our technologies accordingly, discovering in the process a vast opportunity of learning and shared prosperity? This can be a huge and difficult adventure that will bring out the magnificence of human beings. It is also an act of love and compassion worthy of the earth—an unparalleled rousing of human minds in lifted awareness of our shared reality and shared planet. Transition away from the dream that we can live forever by massive damage to the earth is inevitable. We can do all we can to ensure that this transition is politic, able to take the great majority of us with it to a saner understanding of what a good life might be, in the little time available. We'll still have to pay every part of the price wrought by the changed climatic circumstances already incurred, but we can at least work to ameliorate them and avoid the truly unpayable price of continuing to pretend that this collective fantasy can endure.

A POWERFUL REBELLION OF THE HEART

The transition begins in a rebellion of the heart and the waking up of awareness that is inherent in us all.

Perhaps it begins in noticing a growing repulsion towards the very excess itself. Do we really need more i-gadgets, apps, accessories, fashion items, short-lived toys, supersize servings, outsize cars, huge houses, and double garages bulging with all the things we have grown tired of? A rebellious refusal rises in the heart towards such a shallow, narrow, and essentially *dull* idea of what a human being is.

Or it may start in fury at the growing gulf between rich and poor, the behavior of the banks in privatizing every cent of their massive profit while nationalizing their trillion dollar losses through public bail-outs by the same taxpayers whose life savings and homes they gambled and profiteered away. Or in the despair of being young, educated, saddled with a huge education debt, but with no prospect of work. Or in the grief of seeing old-growth forests clear-felled for disposable chopsticks and paper packaging, or burned to make way for palm oil plantations, dispossessing the last orangutans of their remnant ecological niche.

One playful Zen *koan*, shaped to kick-start our startling left-of-field heartfelt intelligence, goes like this: "Once, a woman raised a goose inside a bottle. When the goose was grown, she wanted to get it out. How do you free the goose without breaking the bottle?"

How *do* you break free the human mindset that has trapped us, become toxic, and begun eating the earth alive? Now that question is still too full of the thinking that created the problem. There's a self-imposed barrier in proposing a problem of breaking free, since original freedom might well be discoverable as the very nature of the one who asks. To get down to that you have to first let go of all you think you know about "glass," "bottles," and "goose." "So where do you find your self?" asked Yunmen, so casually you might think he was not urging you to break out of prison.

How will we avoid shattering human life into post-apocalyptic shards of its former self? An immensely practical and important question, yet this *koan* is also asking us to rediscover our original undividedness, and the freedom it bestows, right there in the suffocating fear itself. It invites you to glimpse what the kitchen table moment revealed, that the crisis and salvation are inside each other. Or, as Yunmen put it, "Medicine and sickness heal each other."

Change like this doesn't come from a top-down approach. No living system has a boss. The boss is all of us, inextricably together, using the distributive wisdom of countless local actions occurring simultaneously.

At a practical level, ways of freeing the goose without breaking the bottle can be seen in some of the communal intelligence of nonviolent resistance emerging recently in the Occupy and Indignado movements. I have caught glimpses of the freed goose right there in the inventive energy of those recent uprisings. To be able to realize our real freedom within a sober, creative, playful awareness of reality is vital to get beyond the thinking that created the problem. Even if one in a hundred people begin to wake up to this degree, change ripples through, person to person, exactly like the Occupy Wall Street's "people's microphone," created to pass words of a public address from person to person when the right to using a public address system was denied.

As William James said, countless small acts wear down the mighty when they simply persist in going under, over, or around every barrier placed in their path, or act from seeing right through them, in the spirit of the Zen *koan*. The ancient Taoist text, the *Daodejing*, which foreshadows and influences much of the character of Chinese Zen, says the same thing in the form of a fine *koan* for our time: "The softest thing on earth overtakes the hardest thing on earth."

It is almost as though we need to relearn the fundamentals that once were natural to us, like someone recovering from brain trauma: what it means to be a human being, a member of society, part of a family and a community, and of the great community of life, in literally remembering what *planet* we're on. Can we quiet our nerves and minds for a time, look deep inside our own humanity and our natures to rediscover the medicine to heal our collective madness? For we're not dead yet, and the world is still alive to sensitive human touch, so long as we extend it.

And when the stakes are life on earth, all else is a diversion.

The same stream of life that runs
through my veins night and day runs
through the world and dances in rhythmic measures.

It is the same life that shoots in joy
through the dust of the earth in numberless blades of grass and
breaks into tumultuous waves of leaves and flowers.

It is the same life that is rocked in the ocean-cradle
of birth and of death, in ebb and in flow.

I feel my limbs are made glorious by the touch of this world
of life. And my pride is from the life-throb of ages
dancing in my blood this moment.

RABINDRANATH TAGORE,
Gitanjali, LXIX

SATISH KUMAR *has walked the Earth to spiritually connect with nature, which he describes as his guide and cathedral. Editor of* Resurgence Magazine *and guiding spirit behind Schumacher College, he insists that we reaffirm the spiritual aspect of the environment. Reverence for nature needs be at the heart of our political and social debate.*

Three Dimensions of Ecology: Soil, Soul and Society

SATISH KUMAR

GREAT MOVEMENTS and perennial philosophies have often summarized their essential messages in trinities. One of the Hindu trinities is Brahman, Vishnu and Shiva—the principles of creation, continuity and decay. Christians have the Father, the Son and the Holy Spirit. The Greeks focussed on truth, goodness and beauty. The American Constitution came up with life, liberty and the pursuit of happiness and the French Revolution with liberty, equality and fraternity. In our own time, the new-age movement gathered around the concepts of mind, body and spirit. These trinities have their point and are relevant in their own context but none of them represents a holistic and ecological worldview. They are either spiritual or social but they are anthropocentric and fail to highlight the human/nature connection.

However, an ancient Hindu text, the *Bhagavad Gita*, contains a trinity which in my view is holistic, and inclusive of ecology, spirituality and humanity. That trinity in Sanskrit is *yagna, tapas* and *dana. Yagna* relates to human/nature relationships, *tapas* relates to human/divine relationships and *dana* relates to human/human relationships. I have translated this trinity into English as Soil, Soul and Society.

ECOLOGY OF THE SOIL

Soil comes first. It represents nature and sustains the entire world. Everything comes from the soil and returns to the soil. Food which sustains life comes from the soil. Water which nourishes life is held by the soil and so is fire. The sun, the moon and the stars are all related to the soil. For me the soil is a metaphor for the entire natural system. If we take care of the soil, the soil will take care of us all. Through the soil we are all related and interconnected. We depend on the soil. All living beings depend on the soil.

Unfortunately the sciences, technology, economics and philosophy in the past few centuries have developed in such a way that we have elevated humankind to the ruling position and given humans higher status. We have developed a worldview which dictates that the human species is superior to all other species. Animals, forests, rivers and oceans must serve and fulfil not only the needs of humankind but also its greed and desires. This way of thinking has been called species-ism which means that one species, the human species, is the superior species above all others.

This arrogant worldview has led to the demise of reciprocal, mutual, respectful, reverential and spiritual relationships between humans and the rest of nature. In fact humans have come to believe that they are separate from nature and above nature. Nature is out there—the forests, the rivers, the birds and other wildlife—and we humans are here enclosed in our homes, palaces, castles, apartments, offices, cars, trains and airplanes.

In the recent past there have been philosophers and scientists who have considered it right for humanity to go on a mission of conquering nature through technology, science, industry and trade. Humanity has been at war against nature during this industrial and technological age: poisoning the land with chemicals and pesticides in the name of increasing food production. We have put birds and animals in coops and cages and treated them cruelly so that greater and greater profit can be made through increased sale of animal protein. Relentless destruction of rain forest as well as deciduous forest has been justified to increase areas of arable land for agribusiness. The industrial scale of fishing which depletes and destroys the natural balance of the oceans and rivers is another example of our acts of war against nature. Little do we realize that even if we were to win this war we would find ourselves on the losing side.

This war against nature is driven by our conviction that the function of nature is to drive the engine of economy. This must change. The truth of the matter is that economy is a wholly owned subsidiary of ecology or the environment. If the natural capital is depleted—if the environment is destroyed—then the economy will come to an end!

Thus the challenge for humankind, in the twenty-first century, is to find humility and overcome duality and disconnection with nature. Nature is not just out there, we are nature too. Natal, nativity, native and nature all come from the same root. The word nature means: whatever is born and will die. Since we, humans, are also born and will die we are nature too. Thus nature and humans are one. Therefore we need to understand that what we do to nature we do to ourselves. We are all related; we live in an interdependent world.

With this sense of the unity of humans and nature we come to a new way of appreciating and valuing all life. The Norwegian philosopher, Arne Naess, called it deep ecology. When we value nature only in terms of her usefulness to humans, even though we conserve her and protect her for our benefit, it is shallow ecology. But when we recognize the intrinsic value of all life, small or large, then it is deep ecology. A blade of grass, an earthworm, an insect, even a mosquito has the right to life; so have trees, rivers, birds and fish irrespective of their usefulness to humans.

As we have recognized human rights, deep ecology requires us to recognize the rights of nature. Our relationship with nature must be embedded in an increasing awareness of the principles of nonviolence and reverence for life. Deep ecology naturally leads to reverential ecology and spiritual ecology.

Nature is not a dead object. Nature is alive. According to the scientist James Lovelock, who has proposed the theory of Gaia, the earth is a living organism and also according to Hindu philosophy, nature is intelligent and conscious. The elements earth, air, fire and water have divinity intrinsic to them. Hindus talk about the rain god Indra, the wind god Vayu, the fire goddess Agni and the earth goddess Bhumi. They also talk about the sun god, the moon goddess, the god of the Himalayas Shiva, the goddess of water Ganga. In essence god or gods are not separate from nature.

Commenting on the *Gita* the Hindu scholar Vinoba Bhave writes, "All that is around us is nothing but god. He is standing before all of us all the time.... It is the Lord, and the Lord alone, who appears in everything animate and inanimate."[1]

Bhave continues, "God is everywhere in the Universe. As holy rivers, high mountains, serene oceans, tender-hearted cows, noble horses, majestic lions, sweet voiced cuckoos, beautiful peacocks, clean and solitude loving snakes, crows flapping their wings, the upward rising flames, the still stars—He is pervading the whole creation in different forms. We should train our eyes to see Him everywhere."[2]

Nature is divine, sacred and holy as well as abundant. And all the species are fed and nourished through the sacrificial act of life sustaining life. We humans are blessed with the gifts of nature as long as we take from nature what we need to meet our vital requirements, for our survival and for our living. We are offered the gifts of food, water and shelter as long as we receive them with humility and gratitude and without abuse, waste, depletion or pollution. The great Indian leader Mahatma Gandhi said, "Nature provides enough for everybody's need but not enough for even one person's greed." According to him waste is violence, pollution is violence and accumulating possessions which are not essential to living is violence.

Nature is kind, compassionate and generous; she is filled with unconditional love: for example, from a tiny seed grows a great apple tree which produces thousands upon thousands of apples, year after year, after year. The tree never consumes its own apples. It offers fruit without asking anyone for anything in return; it delights all comers with fragrant, sweet, nourishing fruit unconditionally. A saint or a sinner, a peasant or a philosopher, a human or an animal, a bird or a wasp, all are invited to enjoy fruit indiscriminately.

According to the principle of *yagna* we should celebrate the beauty, the abundance and the grandeur of nature by replenishing what we have taken. If we take five trees to build our home we must replenish them by planting fifty trees. If we have taken crops of wheat, rice and vegetables from the land and thus taken some goodness out of the soil we must replenish the soil with manure and compost as well as leave the land fallow after seven years of cultivation, thus offering the land a sabbatical. This is called *yagna*, replenishment, restoration and renewal. Vinoba Bhave writes, "If a hundred of us crowd together in one spot for a day that will spoil the place, pollute the atmosphere, thus harm the nature. We should do something to recoup nature, to restore its balance. It is for this purpose that the institution of *yagna* was created. *Yagna* is intended to reimburse, to put back what we have taken from nature ... to make good the loss is one of the purposes of *yagna*."[3]

Nature seen as an inanimate machine becomes an object of exploitation whereas nature seen as sacred becomes a source of inspiration for the arts, culture, architecture and of course religion. We admire and pay tribute to great artists, like Van Gogh for painting sunflowers, forgetting that sunflowers themselves are great works of divine art stimulating the imagination of the artist. If there were no sunflowers there would be no Van Gogh, and no Monet without lilies in the pond, and no Cézanne without Mont Sainte-Victoire. Artists have always recognized the sacred quality of nature. Now it is imperative that scientists, industrialists and politicians do the same and cease to think of nature as a mere resource for profit.

When we practice humility and gratitude we are able to learn much *from* nature. But we in the anthropocentric, modern civilization learn *about* nature. There is a great deal of difference between learning "from" nature and learning "about" nature. When we learn "about" nature she becomes an object of study, leading to exploitation of her. That is why some scientists have spoken about the human mission "to steal the secrets of nature." But when we learn "from" nature we establish a close relationship with her. Then there is implicit humility and reverence towards the mystery of natural processes.

The great Indian poet Rabindranath Tagore established a school near the city of Kolkata called Shantiniketan, meaning house of peace. There he held classes under mango trees and said to his pupils, "You have two teachers; one, myself, your human teacher, and the other, the tree, under which we sit." Tagore went on, "I can give you intellectual knowledge but you can gain much experience by observing the trees. When knowledge and experience meet, wisdom is born."

When we observe trees we realize how everything is interconnected and interrelated. From the energy of the sun the leaves of the tree create photosynthesis; by the rain trees are nourished; the soil holds the roots. Only connect. The Buddha was enlightened while sitting under a tree.

When we experience nature we develop a deep sense of empathy and love for nature and when we love something we care for it, we conserve it and we protect it.

The current environmental movement is driven by fear of doom and disaster. That cannot be the right motivation for a truly sustainable future. Love and reverence for the earth will automatically result in sustainability, harmony and coherence.

We need to realize that harmony is the most fundamental principle of ecology. Wherever there is a breakdown in harmony there is discord and conflict. Our human responsibility is to restore and maintain harmony. The Iranian Sufi scholar Hossein Ghomshei says that the knowledge of universal harmony is science, the expression and communication of that harmony is the arts and the practice of that harmony in our daily life is religion. Thus there is no conflict between science, the arts and religion; they complement each other. Many of our environmental problems arise because we have put the sciences, the arts and religious practices into different compartments. If we wish to create a sustainable future and mitigate problems of resource depletion, the population explosion and the demise of biodiversity, then we need to create a coherence between the sciences, the arts and religions. This can be achieved through a deep sense of respect for soil, for the earth: to be human is to be humble and practice humility!

ECOLOGY OF THE SOUL

As we are urged by the *Gita* to live in harmony with the natural world, soil, we are also guided to live in harmony with ourselves, with soul. As we are at war with nature we are also at war with ourselves. Making peace with ourselves is a prerequisite for making peace with the earth. And making peace with ourselves means realizing our true nature and being who we are.

Each and every one of us is a unique and special being. As the Sri Lankan art historian Ananda Coomaraswami said, "An artist is not a special kind of person but every person is a special kind of artist." He was talking about the immense potential of every human being. Hindu philosophers have spoken of "*aham Brahmasmi*": "I am Brahman—pure consciousness."

In Sanskrit the word for the individual soul is *atman*, the intimate being, and the word for the universal soul is *paramatman*, the ultimate being or god. Similarly the Sanskrit word for the human individual is *nar* and for the universal being (or god) is *narayan*. In Arabic we find a similar formulation—the individual person is called *khud* and the divine being, god, is *Khuda*—just by adding an "a" the individual is released from his or her narrow identity or ego and is transformed into divine consciousness and united with god.

The way to such an enlightened state is through self-knowledge, selfless service, and the surrender of the ego in favor of the understanding that "I am part of the whole": I am an organ of the earth body, I am a member of the earth community.

Often we are weighed down by the burden of our narrow identities of nationality, race, religion, class, gender and similar other divisive concepts and mental constructs. We become imprisoned in the idea of "I" separate from the other and "mine" separate from the other's. Through universal love we are able to break out of this ego and become part of the eco—making a quantum leap by changing from "g" to "c." The Greek word "eco" is very beautiful. From it we get ecology and economy. Eco or rather Greek *oikos* means home. In the wisdom of Greek philosophers, home is not only where we physically live, our house—with a kitchen, bedroom, bathroom, dining room and living room. The entire planet is our home where 8.7 million species live as members of one household, one family; all species are kith and kin. So home or "eco" is a place of relationships whereas "I" as a separate self or ego is a state of separation, disconnection and isolation. Our soul gets starved in isolation.

When we realize, "I am a microcosm of the macrocosm," then we touch the mind of god, free from narrow identities, liberated from sorrow and separation and free from fear and fragmentation.

Sometimes we become convinced that the world needs saving, so urgently that we force ourselves to work day in and day out to save the planet. As a consequence of this view we neglect our own well-being and suffer from burnout, depression, breakdown of marriage and disillusionment.

Therefore the *Gita* teaches us that there is no need to separate caring for the soil from caring for the soul. We need to do both. The practice of the latter is called *tapas* which means taking time for inner purity, meditation, spirituality and living a life of elegant simplicity. Mahatma Gandhi said, "Be the change you want to see in the world." He believed that there should be integrity between theory and practice, between word and action. Words gain power only when they are backed by a living example. This is why Mahatma Gandhi integrated into his day time for prayer, meditation, solitude, study, gardening, cooking and spinning and considered these activities as essential as negotiating with the British rulers of India, organizing the campaign for independence and working for the removal of untouchability. Thus Mahatma Gandhi was a perfect example of uniting the care of the external world with the care of the internal world. The inner landscape of spirituality and the outer landscape of sustainability are intricately linked. We need to cultivate compassion, seek truth, appreciate beauty and work for self-realization. Thus we can connect outer ecology with inner ecology.

The contemporary environmental movement, in the main, follows the path of empirical science, rational thinking, data collection and external action. This is good as far as it goes but it doesn't go far enough. We need to include care of the soul as a part of care of the planet.

ECOLOGY OF SOCIETY

Care for the soil and the soul needs to be extended to include care for society. In spite of the unprecedented growth in the economy, science, technology and world trade, almost half of humanity is hungry, homeless and ignored.

After the Second World War the president of the US, speaking at the UN, declared that there are two worlds, the developed world and the undeveloped world. The developed world is the world of industry, technology, free trade and consumerism which lifts the living standards of all people and the undeveloped world is the world of agriculture, rural life, local economy and low consumption which keeps people in poverty. The mission of mainstream economists and politicians is to industrialize the world, create economic globalization and allow the free market to solve the problem of undevelopment.

In spite of nearly seventy years of relentless efforts towards industrialization, the suffering of people in the so-called undeveloped countries has continued to increase. Even in China, India and Brazil where governments, industrialists and business leaders sacrifice their cultures and traditions and destroy their natural capital in order to follow the path of modern materialism, the majority of their citizens are still living below the poverty line. Even where living standards have risen, and cars, computers and highways have proliferated, general well-being, human happiness, social cohesion and job satisfaction remain a distant dream.

This new religion of materialism has grown side by side with the growth of militarism. Total expenditure on nuclear and conventional weapons has quadrupled in recent years without any sign of an increase in security or peace. Violence in one form or another, legal wars waged by governments or illegal wars waged by so-called "terrorists" continue to occupy many parts of the world without any resolution of national or international conflicts.

Humanity is not only at war against nature, it is at war against itself: the values of profit, power, control and greed rule the minds of mainstream politicians and industrialists, advertising and misinformation seduce the minds of the majority of people who dream of a lifestyle based in consumerism, comfort and extravagance.

This state of affairs is hardly conducive to a vision of harmony, coherence and well-being. Therefore a strong social movement is needed to establish justice, equality, liberty and freedom, leading to the well-being of all. This cannot be done merely by social engineering or political manoeuvring. It can only be done by a spiritual awakening and a new awareness about mutual care and selfless service. The *Gita* calls it *dana* which means sharing, generosity, giving before taking, rising above self-interest.

In a culture where self-interest is promoted as a paramount value, one would naturally ask why should we give up our self-interest? The *Gita's* answer is, as Vinoba says, "Because we are already highly obliged to society. We were totally defenceless and weak when we were born. It is the society that looked after us and brought us up, we should therefore serve it."[4]

We have inherited great architecture: the Pyramids, the Taj Mahal, the great mosques and cathedrals. We are blessed with so much literature, poetry, music and painting. We are enriched by the great teachings of enlightened masters such as the Buddha, Mohammed, Jesus Christ, Lao Tsu and others. We have been endowed with philosophy, science and technology.

The list of gifts we have received and inherited from our ancestors and our fellow human beings is endless. We are indebted to them. And now it is our own turn to contribute to that culture and civilization and ensure that no child in our human family goes without food, no sick person is left unattended, no country or community is afflicted by war, exploitation or torture. We may not achieve this goal tomorrow but efforts towards the well-being of all must start today and we must rise above the narrow confines of self-interest and work towards mutual interest.

But that vision of working for mutual interest is never easy. There are vested interests in society which prevent us from acting in mutual interest and push us towards self-interest. The strong exploit the weak, the rich keep the poor down, seekers of power subjugate the powerless. In such a situation the *Gita* advocates struggle and action.

Mahatma Gandhi was one of the most ardent followers of *Gita* principles. He happily went to prison "like a bridegroom goes to the wedding chamber." He practiced non-violence, truth and compassion, yet fought a battle against colonization and for freedom.

Activists such as Martin Luther King, Nelson Mandela, Vaclav Havel, Mother Theresa and Wangari Maathai are examples of people who acted in the spirit of the *Gita* offering their lives as *dana* for the well-being of society as a whole. From these outstanding activists we can learn the lessons of social ecology and strive to establish a new moral order of human dignity.

So the way of the *Gita* is the way of a spiritual warrior, a peace warrior and an eco-warrior—what *Gita* calls a *karma-yogi:* one who is engaged constantly for the upliftment and well-being of the deprived and dispossessed but who acts without desiring the fruit of his or her own actions. The *Gita* says that as the tree does not eat its own fruit and the river does not drink its own water, the *karma-yogi* should not seek any benefit of his or her own action. Rather he or she should offer that action for the benefit of others. That is *dana.*

The trinity of the *Bhagavad Gita* is like the three legs of a stool: through *yagna* we replenish the soil, through *tapas* we replenish the soul and through *dana* we replenish society. But they are not mutually exclusive. All of us need to engage in all three types of action simultaneously. In a nutshell, we need to live a spiritual way of life and engage in the protection of the earth, enlightenment of the self and restoration of social justice. This ancient trinity of *Gita* is as relevant today as it ever was.

The valley spirit never dies;
It is the woman, primal mother.
Her gateway is the root of heaven and earth.
It is like a veil barely seen.
Use it; it will never fail.

Lao Tsu, *Tao Te Ching*

JOANNA MACY, *eco-philosopher and spiritual activist, returns our notion of the self to a deep kinship with all of life. Combining Buddhism and general systems theory, she expands our story to an ecological self which recognizes that the world is its body.*

The Greening of the Self
JOANNA MACY

May we turn inwards and stumble upon our true roots
in the intertwining biology of this exquisite planet.
May nourishment and power pulse through these roots,
and fierce determination to continue the billion-year dance.
— JOHN SEED

SOMETHING IMPORTANT is happening in our world that you will not read about in the newspapers. I consider it the most fascinating and hopeful development of our time, and it is one of the reasons I am so glad to be alive today. It has to do with our notion of the self.

The self is the metaphoric construct of identity and agency, the hypothetical piece of turf on which we construct our strategies for survival, the notion around which we focus our instincts for self-preservation, our needs for self-approval, and the boundaries of our self-interest. Something is shifting here. The conventional notion of the self with which we have been raised and to which we have been conditioned by mainstream culture is being undermined. What Alan Watts called "the skin-encapsulated ego" and Gregory Bateson referred to as "the epistemological error of Occidental civilization" is being peeled off. It is being replaced by wider constructs of identity and self-interest—by what philosopher Arne Naess termed the ecological self, co-extensive with other beings and the life of our planet. It is what I like to call "the greening of the self."

BODHISATTVAS IN RUBBER BOATS

In a lecture on a college campus some years back, I gave examples of activities being undertaken in defense of life on Earth—actions in which people risk their comfort and even their lives to protect other species. In the Chipko or tree-hugging movement in north India, for example, villagers protect their remaining woodlands from ax and bulldozer by interposing their bodies. On the open seas, Greenpeace activists intervene to protect marine mammals from slaughter. After that talk, I received a letter from a student I'll call Michael. He wrote:

> I think of the tree-huggers hugging my trunk, blocking the chain saws with their bodies. I feel their fingers digging into my bark to stop the steel and let me breathe. I hear the *bodhisattvas* in their rubber boats as they put themselves between the harpoons and me, so I can escape to the depths of the sea. I give thanks for your life and mine, and for life itself. I give thanks for realizing that I too have the powers of the tree-huggers and the *bodhisattvas*.

What is most striking about Michael's words is the shift in identification. Michael is able to extend his sense of self to encompass the self of the tree and of the whale. Tree and whale are no longer removed, separate, disposable objects pertaining to a world "out there"; they are intrinsic to his own vitality. Through the power of his caring, his experience of self is expanded far beyond that skin-encapsulated ego. I quote Michael's words not because they are unusual, but to the contrary, because they express a desire and a capacity that is being released from the prison-cell of old constructs of self. This desire and capacity are arising in more and more people today, out of deep concern for what is happening to our world, as they begin to speak and act on its behalf.

Among those who are shedding these old constructs of self, like old skin of a confining shell, is John Seed, director of the Rainforest Information Center in Australia. One day we were walking through the rain forest in New South Wales, where he has his office, and I asked him: "You talk about the struggle against the lumber companies and politicians to save the remaining rain forests. How do you deal with the despair?"

He replied, "I try to remember that it's not me, John Seed, trying to protect the rain forest. Rather, I am part of the rain forest protecting itself. I am that part of the rain forest recently emerged into human thinking." This is what I mean by the greening of the self. It involves a combining of the mystical with the pragmatic, transcending separateness, alienation, and fragmentation. It is a shift that Seed himself calls "a spiritual change," generating a sense of profound interconnectedness with all life.

This is hardly new to our species. In the past, poets and mystics have been speaking and writing about these ideas, but not people on the barricades agitating for social change. Now the sense of an encompassing self, that deep identity with the wider reaches of life, is a motivation for action. It is a source of courage that helps us stand up to the powers that are still, through force of inertia, working for the destruction of our world. This expanded sense of self leads to sustained and resilient action on behalf of life.

When you look at what is happening to our world—and it is hard to look at what is happening to our water, our air, our trees, our fellow species—it becomes clear that unless you have some roots in a spiritual practice that holds life sacred and encourages joyful communion with all your fellow beings, facing the enormous challenges ahead becomes nearly impossible.

Robert Bellah's book *Habits of the Heart* is not a place where you are going to read about the greening of the self. But it is where you will read *why* there has to be a greening of the self, because it describes the cramp that our society has gotten itself into. Bellah points out that the individualism embodied in and inflamed by the industrial growth society is accelerating. It not only causes alienation and fragmentation in our century but also is endangering our survival. Bellah calls for a moral ecology. "We must have to treat others as part of who we are," he says, "rather than as a 'them' with whom we are in constant competition."

To Robert Bellah, I respond, "It is happening." It is happening because of three converging developments. First, the conventional small self, or ego-self, is being psychologically and spiritually challenged by confrontation with dangers of mass annihilation. The second force working to dismantle the ego-self is a way of seeing that has arisen out of science. From living systems theory and systems cybernetics emerges a process view of the self as inseparable from the web of relationships that sustain it. The third force is the resurgence in our time of non-dualistic spiritualities. Here I write from my own experience with Buddhism, but I also see it happening in other faith traditions, such as the Jewish Renewal Movement, Creation Spirituality in Christianity, and Sufism in Islam, as well as in the appreciation being given to the message of indigenous cultures. These developments are impinging on the self in ways that are helping it to break out of its old boundaries and definition.

CRACKED OPEN BY GRIEF

The move to a wider, ecological sense of self is in large part a function of the dangers that threaten to overwhelm us. Given news reports pointing to the progressive destruction of our biosphere, awareness grows that the world as we know it may come to an end. The loss of certainty that there will be a future is, I believe, the pivotal psychological reality of our time. Why do I claim that this erodes the old sense of self? Because once we stop denying the crises of our time and let ourselves experience the depth of our own responses to the pain of our world—whether it is the burning of the Amazon rain forest, the famines of Africa, or the homeless in our own cities—the grief or anger or fear we experience cannot be reduced to concerns for our own individual skin. When we mourn the destruction of our biosphere, it is categorically distinct from grief at the prospect of our own personal death.

Planetary anguish lifts us onto another systemic level where we open to collective experience. It enables us to recognize our profound interconnectedness with all beings. Don't apologize if you cry for the burning of the Amazon or the Appalachian mountains stripped open for coal. The sorrow, grief, and rage you feel are a measure of your humanity and your evolutionary maturity. As your heart breaks open there will be room for the world to heal. That is what is happening as we see people honestly confronting the sorrows of our time. And it is an adaptive response.

The crisis that threatens our planet, whether seen in its military, ecological, or social aspects, derives from a dysfunctional and pathological notion of the self. It derives from a mistake about our place in the order of things. It is the delusion that the self is so separate and fragile that we must delineate and defend its boundaries; that it is so small and so needy that we must endlessly acquire and endlessly consume; and that as individuals, corporations, nation-states, or a species, we can be immune to what we do to other beings.

The urge to move beyond such a constricted view of self is not new, of course. Many have felt the imperative to extend their self-interest to embrace the whole. What is notable in our situation is that this extension of identity comes not through a desire to be good or altruistic, but simply to be present and own our pain. And that is why this shift in the sense of self is credible to people. As the poet Theodore Roethke said, "I believe my pain."

CYBERNETICS OF THE SELF

Twentieth-century science undermined the notion of a self that is distinct from the world it observes and acts upon. Einstein showed that the self's perceptions are determined by its position in relation to other phenomena. And Heisenberg, in his Uncertainty Principle, demonstrated that its perceptions are changed by the very act of observation.

Systems science goes further in challenging old assumptions about a separate, continuous self, by showing that there is no logical or scientific basis for construing one part of the experienced world as "me" and the rest as "other." That is so because as open, self-organizing systems, our very breathing, acting, and thinking arise in interaction with our shared world through the currents of matter, energy, and information that move through us and sustain us. In the web of relationships that sustain these activities there is no line of demarcation.

As systems theorists say, there is no categorical "I" set over against a categorical "you" or "it." One of the clearest expositions of this is found in the writings of Gregory Bateson, who says that the process that decides and acts cannot be neatly identified with the isolated subjectivity of the individual or located within the confines of the skin. He contends that "the total self-corrective unit that processes information is a system whose boundaries do not at all coincide with the boundaries either of the body or what is popularly called 'self' or 'consciousness.'" He goes on to say, "The self as ordinarily understood is only a small part of a much larger trial-and-error system which does the thinking, acting, and deciding."

Bateson offers two helpful examples. One is a woodcutter in the process of felling a tree. His hands grip the handle of the ax, there is the head of the ax, the trunk of the tree. Whump, he makes a cut. And then whump, another cut. What is the feedback circuit, where is the information that is guiding that cutting down of the tree? It is a whole circle; you can begin at any point. It moves from the eye of the woodcutter, to the hand, to the ax, and back to the cut in the tree. That self-correcting unit is what is chopping down the tree.

In another illustration, a blind person with a cane is walking along the sidewalk. Tap, tap, whoops, there's a fire hydrant, there's a curb. Who is doing the walking? Where is the self of the blind person? What is doing the perceiving and deciding? The self-corrective feedback circuit includes the arm, the hand, the cane, the curb, and the ear. At that moment, that is the self that is walking. Bateson points out that the self is a false reification of an improperly delimited part of a much larger field of interlocking processes. And he goes on to maintain that "this false reification of the self is basic to the planetary ecological crisis in which we find ourselves. We have imagined that we are a unit of survival and we have to see to our own survival, and we imagine that the unit of survival is the separate individual or a separate species, whereas in reality, through the history of evolution it is the individual plus the environment, the species plus the environment, for they are essentially symbiotic."

The self is a metaphor. We can choose to limit it to our skin, our person, our family, our organization, or our species. We can select its boundaries in objective reality. As Bateson explains, our self-reflective purposive consciousness illuminates but a small arc in the currents and loops of knowing that interweave us. It is just as plausible to conceive of mind as coexistent with these larger circuits, with the entire "pattern that connects."

Do not think that to broaden the construct of self in this way will eclipse your distinctiveness or that you will lose your identity like a drop in the ocean. From the systems perspective, the emergence of larger self-organizing patterns and wholes both requires diversity and generates it in turn. Integration and differentiation go hand in hand. "As you let life live through you," poet Roger Keyes says, you just become "more of who you really are."

SPIRITUAL BREAKTHROUGHS

The third factor that helps dismantle the conventional notion of the self as small and separate is the resurgence of nondualistic spiritualities. This trend can be found in all faith traditions. I have found Buddhism to be distinctive for the clarity and sophistication it brings to understanding the dynamics of the self. In much the same way as systems theory does, Buddhism undermines the dichotomy between self and other and belies the concept of a continuous, self-existent entity. It then goes further than systems theory in showing the pathogenic character of any reifications of the self. It goes further still in offering methods for transcending these difficulties and healing this suffering. What the Buddha woke up to under the bodhi tree was *paticca samuppada*: the dependent co-arising of all phenomena, in which you cannot isolate a separate, continuous self.

Over the eons, in every religion, we have wondered: "What do we do with the self, this clamorous 'I,' always wanting attention, always wanting its goodies? Should we crucify, sacrifice, and mortify it? Or should we affirm, improve, and ennoble it?"

The Buddhist path leads us to realize that all we need to do with the self is see through it. It's just a convention, a convenient convention, to be sure, but with no greater reality than that. When you take it too seriously, when you suppose that it is something enduring which you have to defend and promote, it becomes the foundation of delusion, the motive behind our attachments and aversions.

For a beautiful illustration of how this works in a positive feedback loop, consider the Tibetan wheel of life. Pictured there are the various realms of beings, and at the center of that wheel of *samsara* are three figures: the snake, the rooster, and the pig—delusion, greed, and aversion—and they just chase each other round and round. The linchpin is the notion of our self, the notion that we have to protect that self or promote it or do *something* with it.

Oh, the sweetness of realizing: I am not other than what I'm experiencing. I am this breathing. I am this moment, and it is changing, continually arising in the fountain of life. We are not doomed to the perpetual rat race of self-protection and self-advancement. The vicious circle can be broken by the wisdom, *prajna*, of seeing that "self" is just an idea: by the practice of meditation, *dhyana*, which sustains that insight, and by the practice of morality, *sila*, where attention to our actions can free them from bondage to a separate self. Far from the nihilism and escapism often imputed to the Buddhist path, this liberation puts one *into* the world with a livelier sense of social engagement.

Our pain for the world reveals our true nature as one with the entirety of life. The one who knows that is the *bodhisattva*—and we're all capable of it. Each one can recognize and act upon our inter-existence with all beings. When we turn our eyes away from that homeless figure, are we indifferent or is the pain of seeing him or her too great? Do not be easily duped about the apparent indifference of those around you. What looks like apathy is really fear of suffering. But the *bodhisattva* knows that if you're afraid to get close to the pain of our world you'll be banished from its joy as well.

One thing I love about the ecological self is that it makes moral exhortation irrelevant. Sermonizing is both boring and ineffective. This is pointed out by Arne Naess, the Norwegian philosopher, who coined the terms "deep ecology" and "ecological self."

Naess explains that we change the way we experience our self through an ever-widening process of identification. Borrowing from the Hindu tradition, he calls this process *self-realization*: a progression "where the self to be realized extends further and further beyond the separate ego and includes more and more of the phenomenal world." And he says:

> In this process, notions such as altruism and moral duty are left behind. It is tacitly based on the Latin term "ego" which has as its opposite the "alter." Altruism implies that the ego sacrifices its interests in favor of the other, the *alter*. The motivation is primarily that of duty. It is said we *ought* to love others as strongly as we love our self. There are, however, very limited numbers among humanity capable of loving from mere duty or from moral exhortation.
>
> Unfortunately, the extensive moralizing within the ecological movement has given the public the false impression that they are being asked to make a sacrifice—to show more responsibility, more concern, and a nicer moral standard. But all of that would flow naturally and easily if the self were widened

and deepened so that the protection of nature was
felt and perceived as protection of our very selves.

Note that virtue is *not* required. The emergence of the
ecological self, at this point in our history, is required precisely
because moral exhortation does not work. Sermons seldom
hinder us from following our self-interest as we conceive it.

The obvious choice, then, is to extend our notions of
self-interest. For example, it would not occur to me to plead
with you, "Don't saw off your leg. That would be an act of
violence." It wouldn't occur to me (or to you), because your
leg is part of your body. Well, so are the trees in the Amazon
rain basin. They are our external lungs. We are beginning
to realize that the world is our body.

The ecological self, like any notion of selfhood, is a
metaphoric construct, useful for what it allows us to perceive
and how it helps us to behave. It is dynamic and situational,
a perspective we can choose to adopt according to context
and need. Note the words: we can choose. Because it's a
metaphor and not a rigid category, choices can be made to
identify at different moments, with different dimensions or
aspects of our systemically interrelated existence—be they
dying rivers or stranded refugees or the planet itself. In doing
this, the extended self brings into play wider resources—like
a nerve cell in a neural net opening to the charge of the other
neurons. With this extension comes a sense of buoyancy and
resilience. From the wider web in which we take life, inner
resources—courage, endurance, ingenuity—flow through
us if we let them. They come like an unexpected blessing.

By expanding our self-interest to include other beings
in the body of Earth, the ecological self also widens our
window on time. It enlarges our temporal context, freeing
us from identifying our goals and rewards solely in terms of
our present lifetime. The life pouring through us, pumping

our heart and breathing through our lungs, did not begin at our birth or conception. Like every particle in every atom and molecule of our bodies, it goes back through time to the first splitting and spinning of the stars.

Thus the greening of the self helps us to reinhabit time and own our story as life on Earth. We were present in the primal flaring forth, and in the rains that streamed down on this still-molten planet, and in the primordial seas. In our mother's womb we remembered that journey, wearing vestigial gills and tail and fins for hands. Beneath the outer layers of our neocortex and what we learned in school, that story is in us—the story of a deep kinship with all life, bringing strengths that we never imagined. When we claim this story as our innermost sense of who we are, a gladness comes that will help us to survive.

"Nature, psyche, and life appear to me like divinity unfolded—what more could I ask for?"

C.G. JUNG, *The Earth Has a Soul*

"Imagination is the living power and prime agent of all human perception, and is a repetition in the finite mind of the eternal act of creation in the infinite I am."

SAMUEL TAYLOR COLERIDGE

GENEEN MARIE HAUGEN, *wilderness wanderer, scholar, and guide to the intertwined mysteries of nature and psyche, returns us to the wonder of an ensouled world. She reminds us of the use of imagination as a way to enter the enchanted reality of real communion with nature.*

Imagining Earth
GENEEN MARIE HAUGEN

IF WE APPROACHED rivers, mountains, dragonflies, redwoods, and reptiles *as if* all are alive, intelligent, suffused with soul, imagination, and purpose, what might the world become? Who would we become if we participated intentionally with such an animate Earth? Would the world quicken with life if we taught our children—and ourselves!—to sing and celebrate the stories embedded in the body of Earth, in the granite bones of mountains and rainy sky tears, in trembling volcanic bellies and green scented hills? What if we apprehended that by nourishing the land and creatures with generous praise and gratitude, with our remembrance or tears, we rejuvenate our own relationship with the wild Earth, and possibly revitalize the *anima mundi*—or soul of the world?

These were questions I posed to a group of environmental education graduate students during a conversation about Aboriginal Australian songlines—the stories of totemic ancestral journeys imprinted into the land during the Dreamtime, stories that are at once profoundly mythic and, according to at least one researcher, imbued with a deep sense of ecology. Traditional belief suggests that singing or dancing the songlines keeps the land alive. I hoped to fire up the students' imaginations with the possibility that even contemporary Western people like us might "hear" the layered geo-poetry and bio-mythos of the land and inhabitants, and honor them with spoken praise, or song, or dance. Or even—and perhaps especially—grief for what the wild Earth has endured at our hands.

"Isn't that a little contrived?" one student asked. "It doesn't feel comfortable to talk to trees or the river."

True enough, I agreed. It's difficult for Western adults to even imagine that stone or water, forests or creatures, have their own ancestral stories—epic journeys and transformations that are not necessarily the stories we tell about them. It's even more difficult, perhaps, for us to imagine engaging with those stories, participating with our words, gifts, music, or gesture. But what if, I asked, we simply practiced honoring the wild Others *as if* they could hear us, as if they were responsive, and as if Earth depended on this reciprocity for continued flourishing?

"Well," one of the students allowed, "it would be a different world."

TOWARD AN ANIMATE WORLD

A sense of the world's numinous, animating dimension, its psyche or soul—its *anima mundi*—began to recede from the minds of Western people centuries ago. The modern scientific and industrial enterprise is based upon the Cartesian severance of psyche from matter—how else would we bear vivisection, mountaintop removal, rivers poisoned with effluents? Most never questioned the common view that the world is made up of dead or insentient matter, even though our own senses and experiences might sometimes suggest otherwise. For contemporary people, expressing the possibility (or certainty) that there is sentience, psyche, or soul present in everything can be socially risky though not life-threatening, but when radical cosmologist Giordano Bruno affirmed the animate nature of all matter in the sixteenth century, he was burned at the stake for beliefs that challenged the divinely ordained authority of the Medieval Church.[1] With Bruno's execution, and with the loss of so many other human and other-than-human beings, the *anima mundi*—uncelebrated, dishonored—slipped further into the shadows.

James Hillman writes of the need for psychology to return psychic depths to the world, without which we have been trying to heal or treat individual human patients without recognizing sentience—and suffering—in the world in which our individual lives are embedded.[2] It is not clear to me that the world has actually lost its psychic depths, but surely there are few among us who, like Thomas Berry, recognize that the world is saturated in psyche—that "the universe from the beginning has been a psychic-spiritual, as well as a physical-material, reality."[3]

We generally regard our bodies as *ours*, distinct from what is outside our skin, yet our bodies depend on air, water, sunlight—and food, which in turn depends on air, water, sunlight, food. The elements of our bodies were born in a primeval supernova billions of years ago. Who can be sure where our bodies begin or end?

The familiar view suggests that psyche is entirely subjective, residing in the gray matter of the individual brain; yet can we be confident of making the cut that isolates our "own" psyche, mind, or imagination from the larger psyche of the world when we dream of communicating with animals, or of landscapes we have never seen, or when we have a sudden intuition about a distant beloved, or when we have visionary experience, or "remember" lives we have not lived? When we recognize that our animal companions dream, have memory, and sometimes know when we are within miles or hours of arriving home, or when we are aware that plants may respond to our affections, can we be certain that psychic depths are limited to human beings? And even though, by now, the idea of the interconnected body-mind-soul has permeated the "new age" (and beyond), how often do we enact our lives accordingly, as if there is intimate relationship between our imaginations or mental habits and our bodily experience, including our experiences in the embodied, ensouled world beyond ourselves?

IMAGINATION AS THRESHOLD

At dawn in summer, I carry my flute to the top of the slickrock mesa, where the undulating stone summit overlooks valleys, canyons, distant ridges, and peaks. I play the walnut flute as a way of beginning the day, greeting the world, offering melodies to rock, clouds, ponderosa, cottonwood in the draw below, grasses in the fields, meadowlarks, doves, finches, lizards. I play as if there are listeners. The music is simple, untrained. Sometimes I get lost in the rhythm of my breath moving through the flute body, emerging as music, and other times I am keenly aware of the Others, my companions in the dazzling world.

I have been teaching myself this practice of offering small beauty in reciprocity to the world, a practice that is deepened each time I play as if creatures other than human beings might hear me. It is an enormous act of imagination to participate as if even stone "hears" and plays a part in the land's organs of perception. I began many years ago engaging with the world as if it mattered to the Others as well as to me; I began with whispers, with gentle touches, then with praise, poetry, song—actively imagining that it did matter, somehow, even if there was no apparent response. But such offerings brought me more alive, and perhaps opened some hidden organ of perception in me, because the world in which I am embedded seemed to tremble with greater aliveness too, like the sudden greening that follows desert rain.

I want to inhabit a fully animate world—and sometimes I do, although not usually while paying bills or getting the tires rotated. In fact, the animate Earth seldom reaches me when I'm involved in the tasks of maintaining a twenty-first-century life. The laptop seldom speaks, the espresso pot is silent. Even the stones, antlers, and feathers gathered on sills and shelves are mute. But perhaps the world itself does not change; perhaps the *anima mundi* is always near and receptive; perhaps only the lens with which I perceive the world shifts or widens. Engaging with the exuberant wild Earth from a different, deeply imaginative mode of participating consciousness might be something like donning 3-D glasses—a shimmering new dimension is revealed, and it is not just visual. The numinous, psychic atmosphere pulses with aliveness, crackles with curiosity.

Can contemporary Western people reopen the gates of perception to an intelligent, meaningful cosmos, the cosmos as experienced by "nature mystics" and many traditional people—perhaps even our own distant ancestors? If we cultivate the imaginative consciousness that allows for experience and perception of the *anima mundi*, would we be able to continue shutting down Earth's life support systems? Would people who practiced reciprocity to an animate, intelligent Earth have invented fracking, strip mines, Three Mile Island, or the economies of weapons, massive warfare, and destruction? Maybe. Yet it's difficult to envision how a culture of reciprocity would have first developed the necessary Earth-assailing technology; such things would have been, perhaps, as unimaginable as schemes to demolish our own loved ones would be to contemporary people.

AS IF PARTICIPATION MATTERS

Who would we become if we honored the other-than-human world as if it matters to them and to us? If we do not already recognize that the Others are spiritual-psychic presences as well as physical beings, perhaps it's still possible to teach ourselves to sense the world from a different set of assumptions, from a different lens, from a different view.

For most contemporary Western adults, intentionally participating with the other-than-human world requires vivid imagination. But an enchanted world is the natural home of human children. Until the spell is broken, the world sparkles and brims with companions and playmates, daemons and demons. Everything is alive and significant, thrilling, sometimes terrifying. Stones, clouds, and butterflies are capable of conversation. For most Western adults, the spell was broken long ago, and an enchanted worldview of anyone past age six or so is easily dismissed as naïveté, animism, magical thinking, or regarded with suspicion—perhaps mental illness or crackpot mysticism. Yet who does not long, perhaps secretly or with despair, to live in a sentient, meaningful cosmos?

It is one matter to imagine that grass, mountains, Moon, willows, warblers, and weasels are worthy of—and receptive to—our praise and respectful attitudes; it's another matter entirely to deeply believe this, to apprehend out of our own sensate experience that creatures and the body of Earth itself are aware of and in some way responsive to us—and that perhaps they are even participants in human affairs, whether or not we notice. If, as you grew in awareness of the world, you were taught—as children have been taught in many traditional cultures—that the other-than-human world is in conversation with you, asking from you a devoted attention, your experience of the world, your participation, would reflect that foundational understanding. You would be profoundly attuned to the slightest variations in the habits of birds, the arrival of unfamiliar insects, the emergence of rare leaves, the inaudible voice in the forest that says, "wait here." You wait, and in a moment a spotted fawn, or a sow grizzly, pads into view.

A lifetime of such experience would confirm your unshakable belief in communion with an animate, intelligent world.

Even a few such experiences might momentarily assuage the terrible loneliness of living in a meaningless, insentient universe.

APPROACHING THE MYSTERY

In mainstream religious traditions, a creator may be ostensibly worshipped while the creation itself is dishonored; our Western political system and economy are rife with people who claim, for example, allegiance with Judeo-Christian religions yet do not flinch at profiting from the destruction of Earth's life support systems. Reverence is reserved for a disembodied god, or for an afterlife, while the physical universe—the creation itself—is largely regarded as inanimate, dead, a warehouse of senseless objects for exploitation and consumption.

Yet some contemporary people, even now, find the presence of gods or the great mystery in the physical universe itself—in the green genius of photosynthesizers, in the owl carrying a shrew into the sky, in the cosmological epic inscribed in the dark heavens, in the Moon's love dance with tides, in the baffling layers of geological history. "I don't know exactly what a prayer is. / I do know how to pay attention, how to fall down / into the grass, how to kneel down in the grass ..." writes Mary Oliver in "The Summer Day."

Paying attention, kneeling in the grass—these are acts of reciprocity, and who knows but that Earth responds to this loving attention? Perhaps grass knelt upon in reverence, or ecstasy, or even in grief transmits a secret affirming signal to earthworms and microbes, burrowers and fungi. Perhaps a tree whose bark is caressed by kind hands tingles and flushes to its budding tips with nourishing sap. Perhaps the shaggy pregnant bison who hears a soft voice singing registers the sound with quickening rush of blood to her womb.

If we cannot gauge the effect our attentions have on the other-than-human world, if we cannot measure the value to bison or frogs, owls or grass, perhaps we might notice how we ourselves are opened, at least for a moment. How we, for those attentive minutes or seconds or hours, are not the same isolated human being. A practice of attending an animate world may have a cumulative effect of rearranging our own consciousness in a way that we cannot later withdraw from without pain. An experience of sitting in contemplation with prairie grass, for example, may resurge into aliveness later, when we realize we are mindlessly grabbing weedkiller out of the garage in our ordinary campaign on undesirable tenants. A felt-sense of praising the wild stream may become present for us again, later, when we are poised to flush questionable cleaning products down the drain, or when we are heedlessly running water through the tap, our only concern whether it's purified to *our* own standards.

In an intriguing thought experiment, Richard Tarnas invites readers of *Cosmos and Psyche* to imagine that "you are the universe"—an extravagant stretch of almost anyone's imagination, especially to imagine yourself as "a deep-souled, subtly mysterious cosmos of great spiritual beauty and creative intelligence." You, as the intelligent ensouled universe, are approached by two distinctly different suitors who embody radically divergent ways of knowing—or epistemologies— and who presumably want to know you. The two suitors have contrasting approaches, and you have choice. Would you reveal yourself most fully to the suitor who regards you as inferior, controllable, and lacking in purpose, or would you reveal your trembling depths to the suitor "who viewed you as *at least* as intelligent and noble, as worthy a being, as permeated with mind and soul, as imbued with moral aspiration and purpose, as endowed with spiritual depths and mystery" as the suitor?[4]

If the world seems vacant of mystery, without intelligence or feeling, lacking in purpose, absent of psyche, might it be because we step into the world with heavy feet and dulled senses, our imaginations hijacked by corporate advertising, inane "entertainment," mindless screen addictions and media-manufactured fear? Maybe some people thrive in a meaningless, unfeeling universe, on a dead planet whose only purpose is to provide objects for consumption, but I cannot say that I am acquainted with anyone who truly flourishes in such circumstance.

When the culture does not honor or recognize the world as soul-filled, an individual practice of going forth into our lives as if everything is intelligent and participatory is both essential and risky. We may lose friends, or make new ones, or both.

PRACTICE OF ATTENDING

Human beings and many other mammals don't flourish in the absence of affection, but is this response limited to warm-blooded, mammary-glanded, peripatetic creatures like us? If we believed otherwise, would we pass through the world so casually, riveted to the tunnel-vision of human desire? Or would our human inventions be coherent with natural systems—our buildings shaped of local materials, our energy sources ever-renewing, our industries compatible with ecological design? Would our first love with wild iris or bluebirds or rain forest be loyal and enduring, would we sing back to river and wind?

A practice of honoring the other-than-human world—both embodied and numinous—informs me in my work as a guide to the intertwined mysteries of nature and psyche. Approaching the world as if it is alive and intelligent sometimes causes a wobble in ordinary experience and perception, not only for me but sometimes for participants.

Once I had a man in a short program who had a long history of activism on behalf of wild places, particularly the Arctic National Wildlife Refuge, and who considered himself deeply informed about the wild Earth. I invited my group to wander out for a brief solo "conversation" with nature, on a land that held some of the dangers of true wildness—opportunities to get lost, large creatures, including moose and bears—even though the land is no longer truly wild. If you walk far enough in any direction, you will encounter, not far away, a road, a well-worn trail, or a waterway whose direction will be a compass for locating yourself again. But this man returned from his solo time with wide eyes and a bewildered expression. He said that although he'd spent a lot of time in "wilderness," he had never before, not once, been alone—no other human within his range of hearing or vision. He had never before noticed so many phenomena not pointed out to him by a guide or companion; he had never heard the full polyphony of creaking trees, muted wind in the grass, unidentified footfalls through the dark timber, distant purl of water, rapid chatter of squirrels and whistles, trills, and shrieks of birds overhead. Noticing these things—noticing enough to recognize that he was a novice, a beginner, an initiate, still only a visitor, hardly intimate, hardly fluent in a land whose language he barely understood—was perhaps his first true act of intimate reciprocity, his first act of offering his deepest attention to the animate world.

On another day, a woman walked into the forest, offering spoken praise to moss, to Douglas fir and spruce, to the unknown birds flitting in the branches. She listened and waited, walked slowly on, over the carpet of pine needles, elk droppings, and low-growing plants. She moved softly, noticing the sunlight slanting through the green canopy, noticing the shining webs of spiders hanging between limbs, noticing the particular cracks and furrows in the skin of the old trees. She pressed her nose against a certain tree, caressing the brown bark with her bare hands. She stepped into a small clearing and felt her skin prickle, the intelligent rise of hair on the back of the neck. Breathing slowly, she sensed an immense, sentient presence, sensed that she was not only witnessing the inarticulate Others, but that *she was being witnessed.*

Another woman had previously walked in the forest only with the sense of being alien, an intruder, an unwelcome disturbance. She was quite convinced that she and other people have no natural place amidst the wild. Yet her dreams suggested a longing and perhaps even grief about her distance from wild nature—her own wild nature, and the Earth's. During the day, she walked deeper into an image presented in a dream. She took a path toward swampy ground where she covered her hands and face and feet with mud. Whether she intended it or not, the clay secretly did its work, transforming her ordinary edges, blurring the line between the civilized, rational human and primordial self. When—after lingering in the swampy clearing, attentive to the long grasses, the Sun, the perimeter of trees, the insects over the water—she walked into the forest again, mud cracking on her skin and drifting into the air as fine dust, she experienced herself as Earth emerged from Earth.

She recognized herself as Earth, walking.

Sometimes we might experience a sudden, unanticipated rearrangement of consciousness regarding ourselves in relationship to a wider community—a moment of epiphany that may or may not become a watershed, a trail marker, a cairn, for the direction the rest of our life turns. We may even long for such moments, to be touched by a divine *dianoia*— a profound, experiential knowing that shakes, and forever changes, the foundational beliefs that underlie perceptions.

We might be lucky enough to accidentally stumble into such a revelatory experience without preparation, without practice, without planning. An encounter with unfathomable beauty, terminal illness, or any extreme of human experience might induce a sudden shift in consciousness, a sacred *knowing*. But perhaps more commonly, states of non-ordinary perception are first entered with practice— meditation, prayer, chant, trance dance—or perhaps with a sacramental entheogen such as peyote, psilocybin mushrooms, or ayahuasca.

The woman who experienced herself as Earth walking, the woman who experienced a sense of being witnessed by the mute Others, the man who recognized himself as a pilgrim, a novice in the wild world—each walked "deliberately," as Thoreau did, into the meadows, swamp, and forest. Each walked with aroused imagination, as if all the world is alive and participatory. They practiced offering themselves—body and senses, imagination, wonder, attention, and praise. None of them knew in advance that they would be any different upon return. Of course, a single event does not necessarily reorient a life, but a practice of imaginative reciprocity to the animate world is a doorway through which we might slip into experiential, somatic, emotional, psychic knowing that the world is not quite what we previously believed, and that we are not quite who we thought we were.

Revitalizing the soul of the world depends on a conscious, engaged *relationship* between human beings and Earth. If our discernment of *anima mundi* is dim—as it is for most contemporary people—purposeful acts of radical imagination can stir and awaken our perceptions. James Hillman writes that our "imaginative recognition, the childlike act of imagining the world, animates the world and returns it to soul."[5]

Perhaps the world deeply longs for the consciously imagining human to participate in birthing a new era in the human-Earth relationship. A practice of approaching the world *as if* everything is alive—saturated with psyche, purpose, and intelligence—re-enlivens us; in companionship with our increasing human aliveness, the world shimmers with both possibility and pain, no longer insentient, no longer without its own longings, its psychic depths, its soul.

Hymn to Gaia, Mother of All

Gaia, mother of all,
the oldest one, the foundation,
I shall sing to Earth.

She feeds everyone in the world.

Whoever you are,
whether you walk upon her sacred ground
or move through the paths of the sea
you who fly,
it is she who nourishes you
from her treasure-store.

Queen of Earth, through you
beautiful children,
beautiful harvests,
come.

You give life
and you take life away.
Blessed is the one you honor with a willing heart.
They who have this have everything.

Their fields thicken with bright corn,
the cattle grows heavy in the pastures,
their house brims over with good things.

The men are masters of their city,
the laws are just,
the women are fair,
happiness and fortune richly follow them.

Their sons delight in the ecstasy of youth,
their daughters play
they dance in the grass,
skipping in and out
they dance in the grass over soft flowers.

It was you who honored them,
generous goddess, sacred spirit.

Farewell, mother of the gods,
bride of starry Heaven.

For my song, allow me a life
my heart loves.

And now and in another song
I shall remember you.[1]

Jungian analyst, author, and scholar JULES CASHFORD *evokes the archetype of Gaia, goddess of the Earth. She traces the roots of this re-emerging symbol, and explores why Gaia has become a central and numinous figure in our re-imagining of the Earth.*

Gaia & the Anima Mundi
Jules Cashford

A S THOUGH in answer to the crisis and opportunity of
our time, the image of Gaia is appearing everywhere.
At least 2700 years ago, Gaia was the ancient Greek Mother
Goddess, Earth. Yet her name, and the memory of an animate
Earth, has re-entered Western consciousness in the last forty
years, and since then acquired a life of its own. This is just
what we might expect from an image that appears to arise
spontaneously from a region beyond our conscious control—
the region of myth and dream, symbol and metaphor, where
inspiration is breathed into us and imagination "bodies forth
the forms of things unknown,"[2] the place from which life-
changing intuitions come.

C.G. Jung called this dimension of the human psyche
the Collective Unconscious. Jung found that the Collective
Unconscious, and the archetypal images through which it
manifests into consciousness, extend beyond the individual,
beyond even the human, to become the bearer of universal
objective values. As archetypes are images of instincts that
we share with all other living creatures, so the psyche is "also
nature," or "simply nature." Jung proposed that the archetype
of wholeness is not confined to the human Self but embraces
the whole universe. Ultimately, the Collective Unconscious
became for Jung an expression of the *Anima Mundi*, the Soul
of the World.

There have been many metaphors through which our temporal discriminating minds have tried to comprehend the eternal mystery of the One becoming many while being always One. This is the mystery of the Divine becoming immanent as creation while being transcendent to creation, such that the created universe participates in the divinity of the creative source. One of the most beautiful of these metaphors is *Indra's Net,* from the Mahayana Buddhist tradition. There the universe is seen as an infinite net; wherever the threads cross there is a clear shining pearl that reflects and is itself reflected in every other pearl in an infinite pattern of reflections. Each pearl is an individual consciousness—whether of a human being, an animal, a plant, a cell or an atom—so a change in one pearl, however small, makes a change in all the other pearls, each one both singular and responsive to the whole.

In the Gnostic Gospel of Thomas, it is Jesus himself who is "the All": "I am the All," Jesus says. "Cleave a piece of wood and I am there. Lift up the stone and you will find me there."[3] Plato before him envisioned the world as "a living being endowed with soul and intelligence ... a single entity containing all other living entities, which by their nature are all related."[4] For the seventeenth-century Jewish Dutch philosopher Spinoza, "God and Nature are two words for the same substance."

Mystics and poets, among many others, have always perceived the world as a living unity, ensouled with the same life as their own, and though this vision may go underground it never dies out, no matter what the prevailing beliefs of the age may be. In medieval times it was known as the Great Chain of Being; the Alchemists called it the Golden Chain. Aldous Huxley named it the Perennial Philosophy. Chief Seattle saw it as the Great Web of Life: "Man did not weave the web of life. He is merely a strand in it. Whatever he does to the web he does to himself."[5]

W.B. Yeats envisaged this living unity as the "Great Mind" and the "Great Memory," which "renews the world and men's thoughts age after age"; "whatever the passions of man have gathered about becomes a symbol in the Great Memory." As the Memory of Nature herself, the Great Memory was also the *Spiritus Mundi* or *Anima Mundi*. Like the Collective Unconscious, Yeats' Great Memory is not set apart from us, for our memories and dreams are a part of it as it is of us, all indissolubly entwined and so continually if imperceptibly changing. We reach it through our passions, some "mysterious tide in the depths of our being," and we invoke it by engaging with symbols through Imagination. And is not "Imagination ... always seeking to remake the world according to the impulses and the patterns in that Great Mind, and that Great Memory"?[6]

Could it be that "Gaia" is becoming one of those symbols through which Imagination seeks to remake the world according to the pattern of the Great Memory or the *Anima Mundi*?

GAIA AS HYPOTHESIS

The apparent coincidence that brought the image of Gaia back from its distant past was an apparently random walk taken by the physicist James Lovelock in the late 1970s with his friend, the novelist and classicist William Golding. Lovelock was looking for a name for his new hypothesis that the Earth was a self-regulating system. He wanted to propose that the Earth had the capacity for homeostasis—that is, for comprehensive inner adjustment and self-regulation in response to changes in the outer world. Golding suggested "Gaia," the name of the ancient Greek Mother Goddess of All, and the "Gaia Hypothesis" was born.[7]

But no one anticipated that the image of Gaia would catch the Imagination of the time, almost as though it had a mind of its own. The "Gaia Hypothesis" soon became more radical than Lovelock had intended, as if the hypothesis that excited less scientific minds than his own were primarily to do with Gaia herself, with a vision of Earth as alive—not, as in the current view, dead "matter" opposed to "spirit," to be controlled and explained only by mechanistic laws. This "new Gaia" called forth the "old Gaia": both were animate, intelligent, purposeful—in a word, ensouled—more like a Goddess than a machine.

In retrospect, it seems that what appeared as coincidence—of the choice of the name of "Gaia" to describe a scientific hypothesis otherwise known as "systems theory" —could be meaningful at a deeper level. Jung had proposed the idea of "Synchronicity" to point to the way that certain events, happening together at the same time, may be connected not by cause but by meaning. In which case, the intuition of meaning may refer us to a deeper realm that underlies both physical and psychological expressions—those depths where, the poet Rilke says, "all becomes law."[8]

We might expect a new expression of the Soul of the World to become manifest in a numinous image ("numinous," from the Greek, meaning the "nod" of a deity, the coming alive of divine presence). A numinous image *shines* at us, beckons us beyond our habitual categories of perception: it is *"translucent,"* in Coleridge's term, to "the eternal through and in the temporal."[9] This numinous image may also be an old image seen in a new way. It might be numinous precisely because it came from the depths of the Collective Unconscious to compensate for the present imbalance in human consciousness. It could be trying, in its image of a living Earth, to restore harmony to consciousness—that harmony which was Plato's image both of the universe and of the individual soul in perfect attunement with it.

GAIA AS GODDESS

In the infancy of the world, the Soul of the World and the individual human soul were one.[10] There was no separation between them. In ancient Greece, Gaia, Mother Goddess Earth, still embodied this vision as "Mother of the gods, the Oldest One, the Foundation." In the Olympian myth of creation, Gaia was the first being to arise from chaos.[11] As such she is the origin of "cosmos"—literally, an "ordering," a "harmonious whole"—and so provokes the original moment of wonder that made sense of the world and so laid the foundation on which the mind could rest. What else could she be but "Mother of All"?

In the Homeric Hymn to Gaia (written down in 500 BC, though probably sung at ritual festivals for many centuries before that), quoted as the epigraph of this chapter, Gaia was the Mother who brought forth the universe from herself: all her children were children of the universe, formed from her substance, sharing in her sacred source. Yet "gaia" was also the everyday Greek word for "earth"—the soil we dig, the ground we tread upon. Only the capital letter distinguished them. The "earth that gives us grain" was also the "Mother who feeds the world." The early Greek mind could move fluidly between the two terms without having to reach for a different kind of language to explain which one was meant: they were one and the same. So Gaia, as Goddess, globe and ground, was always transparent to the deeper poetic vision. In contemporary terms, Gaia was a vision of the universe as one dynamic living whole—the expression of the Soul of the World.

Astonishingly, this was the last time in the West that the Earth was formally revered as sacred—over two and a half thousand years ago.

GAIA AS SYMBOL

For many of our twenty-first century minds, Gaia, the Goddess, has become a symbol of a new mode of consciousness, sometimes called "Gaia Consciousness," that expresses a reverence for the planet as a living being who is home to all other living beings, *all* of whom share in and give form to her own original and dynamically changing life. In this vision, Earth becomes again a communion of subjects, and a "Thou" who requires from us relationship. It follows that Earth can no longer be seen as dead matter, a collection of objects, an "it"—merely a resource for human beings to plunder at will. She becomes again sacred, as she always was.

The entrance of the image of Gaia in our time is not so unexpected as it might seem. It rests on a sure foundation that has been long preparing itself for change, probably, though rather too slowly, for the last two to four thousand years, ever since numinosity was withdrawn from Mother Earth and transferred first to the Father god of the Heavens (in Babylon, ca. 2000 BC), and then to the transcendent god of Judaic-Christianity, when the feminine principle was doctrinally excluded from the nature of the divine.

In Christian thought, the Virgin Mary has symbolically inherited much of the imaginative range of the earlier Mother Goddesses—she is called "Queen of Heaven," "Star of the Sea (*Stella Maris*)," "Queen of the Underworld." But she is not—nor, doctrinally, could she be—"Queen of Earth," since Earth belongs to the "fallen" universe. Yet it seems there is a movement in the Collective Unconscious to rectify this imbalance. We can trace it, for example, in the call of many millions of people for Mary to play a more essential role in the imagining of the divine Christian order. From her modest appearance in the New Testament, first as the pure vessel and second as a simple loving mother, she has become astonishingly close to being elevated into divinity, to becoming, in image if not doctrine, "a goddess."[12] But because the theology in which the image of Mary was enclosed had not changed, her divinity was again measured by its distance *from* Earth, not its epiphany *as* Earth, so the old antinomies were simply reasserted at a higher level—and the need for an image outside the Christian tradition still remained. Only twenty years later Gaia was to return in an extraordinary union of science and symbol.

Yet the fact that the status of Mary mattered to so many people all over the world appears to validate Jung's claim that "In the Collective Unconscious of the individual, history prepares itself."[13] If we consider that we also are "Gaia"—our consciousness a part of the Earth's consciousness of itself—then is it not possible that, in ways we can barely conceive, this could also be an aspect of the *dynamic self-regulation* of the whole, suggested in the "Gaia Hypothesis"? That, in other words, Gaia works through the Collective Unconscious, or perhaps, more evocatively, that Gaia is the latest expression of the *Anima Mundi*?

This shows us that Gaia, Mother Earth, is within us, as well as outside us. "What is within surrounds us," as Rilke says.[14] Gaia speaks from within us as a compelling urgency to achieve a new responsible relationship to the whole of life of which we are only a part.

In 1972, a new image of the Earth as a whole entered the collective Imagination with the first stunning photographs of Earth taken by the Apollo 17 astronauts, offering an unprecedented perspective on Earth that starts not from ourselves but from the universe—showing us, for the first time, the Earth as a beautiful, luminous whole.

It seems possible to make sense of the resurgence of "Gaia" through this historical pattern. For when Gaia was the Great Mother Earth and clothed in numinosity, humanity was her child and participated in her immanent divinity, as did all her other children. After the long process of withdrawing from, opposing and, in this and the last century, despoiling Nature, it may be that our images are moving us towards the creation of a new mythology, the "mythology of this unified earth as of one harmonious being," as Joseph Campbell phrased it.[15]

A profound sympathy for Gaia as our beautiful living Earth, and a compassion for all of her creatures, might then inspire us towards the next evolutionary phase, one in which Earth, and all who live on Earth, become sacred as before. It is up to us to participate imaginatively with this symbol and this story, and to assist the process of realizing the "one harmonious being," which for so long we, as a species, have disrupted and, ever increasingly, harmed. In this way, perhaps, humankind can live again "the symbolic life" so that the souls of the world and the World Soul might be reunited at a new conscious level through the Imagination.

This vision evokes the words of Albert Einstein:

A human being is part of the whole called by us "the universe," a part limited in time and space. We experience ourselves, our thoughts and feelings, as something separate from the rest—a kind of optical illusion of our consciousness. This delusion is a kind of prison for us, restricting us to our personal desires and affection for a few persons nearest to us. Our task must be to free ourselves from this prison by widening our circle of understanding and compassion to embrace all living creatures and the whole of Nature in its beauty.[16]

There are fiery sparks of the world soul,
of the light of nature, dispersed or sprinkled in
and throughout the structure of the great world
into all the fruits of the elements everywhere.

ALCHEMICAL TEXT

Depth psychologist and initiatory guide BILL PLOTKIN *expands our understanding of soul to our place within the whole Earth community. He writes that if we are to have a healthy human culture, we need to embrace the daunting work of caring for the world soul.*

Care of the Soul of the World
BILL PLOTKIN

HUMANITY'S MOST URGENT and life-enhancing project, especially in the early twenty-first century, is to care for the soul of the world, the *anima mundi*, which we might also call the soul of the Earth or the soul of the more-than-human community.

This chapter is an exploration of the meaning of *anima mundi* and how we might care for the soul of the world. First, let's consider the more fundamental idea of *soul* and then *the human soul*, in particular, and the relationship between the human soul and the soul of the world.

SOUL

By *soul*, I mean a thing's ultimate place in the world. *Every* thing has a particular place in the world, and so everything, in this sense, has a soul—every creature, mountain, river, valley, stone, flower, and child; every book, piano, house, and teacup; every organization, religion, and science. And the Earth, Moon, and Milky Way. Events, too, have souls— each sunset and hurricane, wedding and death. And relationships, too—those between friends, lovers, and family members, between predator and prey, farmer and land, teacher and student.

When I say every thing has a *place*, I mean not its geographical location but the role, function, station, status, or niche it has in relation to other things. A thing's place tells you how it fits in the world. A particular elder, for instance, might have the place in your life of grandmother, teacher, or congresswoman. Elders, in general, might be said to have the place of guardians of nature, culture, and the *anima mundi*.

A thing's *ultimate* place is its place in the great scheme of things, its quintessential place in the world or the Universe. Soul, then, is the place that most centrally and comprehensively identifies a thing—a thing's *truest* place, the very core or heart of a thing's identity, its decisive meaning or significance, its purpose, its *raison d'être*.

The soul of humanity, for example, might be said to be the conscious celebration of the universe's grandeur. The soul of the US Declaration of Independence is perhaps the affirmation of universal human equality (however poorly the US has succeeded at manifesting this so far). The soul of a possible true democracy—or, better, a future biocracy— might be the affirmation of the inalienable rights of all species and all habitats. The soul of Jesus could be said to be love, and the soul of the Buddha, emptiness.

By *human soul*, I mean an individual person's ultimate place in the more-than-human world—his or her place in the Earth community, not just in a human society. This is a mysterious and possibly mystical idea for many people in contemporary Western cultures—that above and beyond social-vocational roles, each person has a unique *ecological* role, a role she was *born* for, a singular way he can serve and nurture the web of life. Coming to understand the nature of this unique ecological role or place is the intended outcome of the now-rare psychospiritual process of soul initiation, a process, typically, of many years.

A person's ultimate place in the world corresponds to her unique identity, her *mythopoetic* identity, one that is revealed and expressed through symbol and metaphor, image and dream, archetype and myth. Or, in a more poetic vein but with the same meaning, soul has been said to be "the largest conversation you're capable of having with the world," "the truth at the center of the image you were born with," "the shape that waits in the seed of you to grow and spread its branches against a future sky," or "your individual puzzle piece in the Great Mystery."[1] Examples:[2] The soul of Irish poet William Butler Yeats might be articulated, by way of a poem he wrote (and an experience he had) in his late twenties, as the niche of one who "pluck[s] the silver apples of the moon, the golden apples of the sun."[3] Ecophilosopher, Buddhist, and Earth elder Joanna Macy, at age thirty-seven, experienced a life-transforming inner image of a stone bridge that spanned "between the thought-worlds of East and West, connecting the insights of the *Buddha Dharma* with the modern Western mind." She knew in that moment that her destiny was, in part, to be one of the stones in that bridge—"just one, that was enough."[4] And it might be said that cultural historian Thomas Berry was ensouled as someone who "preserves and enhances [wildness] in the natural cycles of its transformation" and who perceives, articulates, and advocates the "dream of the Earth."[5]

As your ultimate place, your soul is both yours and the world's. Yes, it's *your* place, but it's also a distinctive place in the world, like a vibrant space of shimmering potential waiting to be discovered, claimed ... occupied. Your soul is in and of the world, like a whirlpool in a river, a wave in the ocean, or a branch of flame in a fire. For this reason, I think of the human soul as being both psychological (mythopoetic) and ecological; it is our individual psycho-ecological niche. Psyche is not separate from nature, not separate from the world; rather, psyche is an attribute of each thing in the world.

If your soul is your ultimate place in the world and you need to live from that place to be fully yourself, then the world cannot be fully *itself* until you become fully *yourself*. Your soul is part of the soul of the world. How we live our lives has a direct effect on the *anima mundi*. The world needs us to recognize its sacredness and to discover and inhabit our sacred roles in its evolutionary unfolding.

The ego—a fragment of an individual human psyche that observes the rest of its psyche from a psychological distance—has limited knowledge about the psyche of which it is a part. When we're young, a virtually universal component of what our ego doesn't know is our ultimate place, our soul. This knowledge is hidden in the depths of the psyche and in the wilds of the world, and it takes a mature ego to find and comprehend it. In contemporary Western societies, most people never find it.

The journey to self-knowledge that we each must take —the conscious discovery of our ultimate individual place —is the prerequisite to full human consciousness, to the full savoring of the grandeur of this world, to the privilege of fully participating in life, and to the responsibility of contributing something sacred and essential to this world.

Wisdom traditions worldwide say there's no greater blessing than to live the life of your soul; doing so is the source of your deepest personal fulfillment and of your greatest service to others. It's what you were born for. It's the locus of authentic personal power—not power *over* people and things, but rather the power of partnership *with* others, the power to co-create and enhance life and to cooperate with an evolving universe.

Before you discover your ultimate place, you are, in a sense, lost. Before soul initiation, in other words, you have a particular destiny but don't know what it is.

Your soul is your true home. In the moment you finally arrive in and occupy this psycho-ecological niche, you feel fully available and present to the world, unlost. This particular place is profoundly familiar to you, more so than any geographical location or any mere dwelling has ever been or could be. You know immediately that *this* is the source, the marrow, of your true belonging. This is the identity no one could ever take from you. Inhabiting this place does not depend on having anyone else's permission or approval or presence. It does not require having a particular job—or any at all. You can be neither hired for it nor fired from it. Acting from this place aligns you with your surest personal powers (your soul powers), your powers of nurturing, transforming, creating; your powers of presence and wonder.

The first time you consciously inhabit your ultimate place and act from your soul is the first time you can say *Here* and really know what it means. You've arrived, at last, at your own center. As long as you stay Here, everywhere you go, geographically or socially, feels like home. Every place becomes Here.

This is the power of place, the power of Here.

AUTHENTIC ADULTS & TRUE ELDERS

An authentic adult is someone who experiences herself, first and foremost, as a member of the Earth community, has encountered her soul (has had a revelatory experience of her unique mythopoetic place in the Earth community, her ultimate place in the more-than-human world), acquired some practical and culturally-effective means for embodying this place among her people, made a commitment to doing so, and is doing it.

A true elder is someone who, after many years of adulthood, consistently occupies his ultimate place without any further effort to do so. This frees him for something with yet greater scope and depth and fulfillment, namely, caring for the soul of the world. He does this by assisting others to prepare for, discover, and embody their souls, and by supporting the more-than-human community of Earth in the evolution of *its* soul.

SPIRIT & ANIMA MUNDI

By *Spirit*, I mean the universal consciousness, intelligence, psyche, or vast imagination that animates the cosmos and everything in it—including ourselves—and in which the psyche of each person participates. Spirit has many names, commonly capitalized, including the Absolute, the Divine, the Tao, the One, God, Allah, Buddha nature, Great Mystery, and the nondual.

Plato wrote about the world soul, which, in Latin, is *anima mundi*, that which gives a living unity to the entire Universe. *Anima mundi*, then, can be another way to speak of what I mean by Spirit. Both *Spirit* and *anima mundi* point to what all people and all things have in common: our shared membership in a single cosmos, each of us a facet of the One Being that contains all.

The idea of the human soul, in contrast, calls us toward our individual and unique relationship to the world. In this sense, *soul* and *Spirit* suggest opposites—the unique versus the universal, that which is approached by way of descent versus that which is approached by way of ascent. Ultimately, however, each soul (each thing in its soul aspect) exists as an expression of Spirit and serves as an agent or emissary for Spirit.

Our individual relationships with Spirit and soul are not contradictory but complementary. A complete spirituality embraces our relationships to both Spirit and soul, not just one or the other. Together these two realms of spirituality form a whole. Either one alone is incomplete.

It's tempting to say that *Spirit* refers to the soul of the Universe, the "ultimate place" of the Universe—and this, in a way, is correct, except that the ultimate place of the Universe is the Universe itself. It has no further context of existence. The Universe is the one thing that is entirely self-referent and self-normative. Spirit, in other words, is a special case of soul, a boundary condition on what we mean by soul.

But when we refer to Spirit as the *anima mundi*, we're placing an intriguing and vital emphasis on the Universe's meaning, its purpose, its *raison d'être*, its essence. There's a great diversity, of course, in the way individuals and traditions understand the Universe's essence, but by speaking of the *anima mundi*, we're boldly announcing that our subject matter is precisely this grand.

THE WORK OF ELDERS

Healthy human cultures care for the soul of the world. Contemporary Western and Westernized cultures—which I call patho-adolescent cultures—lost their capacity to do this many centuries ago.[6] This is the root of the dilemma we face today. An effective response to the multiple crises of our time requires that we learn again to care for the soul of the world, the *anima mundi*.

The difference between caring for the world and caring for the *soul* of the world is the difference between ecology and spiritual ecology (or deep ecology). In patho-adolescent cultures, "caring for the world," when contemplated at all, is understood from a limited and shallow anthropocentric perspective—what best serves humanity in our immediate egocentric needs independent of the needs of other species or peoples or even of our own grandchildren. In contrast, when we place our emphasis and consciousness on the *soul* of the world, we're embracing the world as something sacred, as something that has its own essence, its own purpose and destiny that might very well be different, bigger, and more mysterious than anything we suspect or anything we could understand. The emphasis shifts from our smaller human needs to the world's needs, the world's longing to evolve along its own trajectory. As poet Robinson Jeffers wrote:

> ... I believe this globed earth
> Not all by chance and fortune brings
> forth her broods,
> But feels and chooses. And the Galaxy,
> the firewheel
> On which we are pinned, the whirlwind of stars
> in which our sun is one dust-grain, one
> electron, this giant atom of the universe
> Is not blind force, but fulfils its life and
> intends its courses ...[7]

In a healthy society, caring for the soul of the world is primarily the work of true elders. These are the community members who have the greatest capacity to recognize and comprehend the needs and desires of the world, and to respond wisely. They are the ones who can best guide us by virtue of their capacity to be guided by the world. By listening to the soul of the world, true elders acquire the wisdom, scope, and perspective to assess the relationship between humanity and the larger web of life we're part of—and to guide us in keeping that relationship in balance. As we're seeing now all too plainly, if the human is not in balance with the whole, everything suffers and eventually dies.

Given that true elders are now rare in this world, what can we do? I see three possibilities: We can support the work of the true elders who *do* still exist. We can create, join, and support nongovernmental organizations that perform what we might call the "cultural eldering function" of a healthy society. And we can each tap into the elder dimension of our individual psyches, regardless of what stage of life we're in.

In the remainder of this chapter, when I write of "elders," I mean all three of the above: individual true elders, the cultural eldering function, and the elder capacity within each of us. When I write of "true elders," on the other hand, I'm referring to those rare individuals who are not simply old (and sometimes not so old at all) but rather who have reached the developmental stage in which their ability to hear the world itself and their desire to care for the soul of the world has become their number-one priority, their center of psychological and spiritual gravity.

The elder dimension in all psychologically healthy people evokes within them a fierce defense and impassioned nurturing of the more-than-human world. The elder within us feels her interdependence with all life and how she is, in essence, summoned into existence through her relationships with all other beings. Her heart naturally breaks open over the suffering of the world, and she will go to whatever lengths necessary to protect life, especially at the species and habitat levels.

The elder's foremost desire is for all beings to be allowed their true place, be given the opportunity to embody their souls, so that the world functions in its fullness, in accordance with its comprehensive destiny. The elder sees how each species, each habitat, and each social issue is related to all others. She understands that everything is alive, that it all fits together, and that we are all participants and reflections of the whole.

Through her devoted tending of the web of life and by her advocacy of the rights of all beings, the elder lends to the human community an air of completeness, rightness, tolerance, compassion, and forgiveness. The rarity of these qualities in our world today speaks to both the scarcity of true elders and our compelling need for them.

CARING FOR THE SOUL OF THE EARTH

The soul of the Earth is the essence of the being some call Gaia. To truly know another individual at her depths is to perceive and to know her soul, the ultimate way she fits into the web of life. Earth, too, can be known this way. To perceive the soul of the Earth requires a sense of what Taoists call the way of life, the fact that everything in our world is in relationship to everything else, that nothing is itself without everything else, and that anything that seems to be a distinct thing is actually an element or strand in a larger pattern. It is to sense what the Chinese call *li*, the dynamic patterning of nature, the web of relationships within and throughout the planet.

To truly care for the Earth community, then, we must learn to sense or intuit the soul of the Earth, the underlying pattern of nature expressed through an astounding diversity of forms and species. A full appreciation of the soul of the Earth—beyond the powers of language to adequately express—comes through years of adult soulwork and the resultant personal development. Those who have attained true elderhood are the ones most gifted at understanding the needs and desires of the Earth. True elders can hear the Earth whispering her guidance. Especially at this time of great crisis and transition, it is the Earth's guidance that we most need.

To care for the soul of the Earth is to maintain the equilibrium between the human community (culture) and the larger, more-than-human world (nature). Without a healthy society, humans perish from starvation, disease, exposure, or war (civil or otherwise). Without the preservation of ecological wildness and diversity, humans and many other species perish from the degradation or loss of habitat. Throughout the twentieth century, and now at the beginning of the twenty-first, we have witnessed the grievous neglect of both culture and nature—by most national governments and most large corporations. Our hope currently lies in the leadership and efforts of those who are attuned to the soul of the Earth—individuals, grassroots networks, nongovernmental organizations, and the more local and smaller-scale governments and businesses.

Caring for the soul of the Earth, the *anima mundi*, has many dimensions. Four of them are: (1) defending and nurturing the innocence and wonder of children, (2) mentoring and initiating adolescents, (3) guiding the evolution or transformation of the culture, and (4) maintaining the balance between human culture and the greater Earth community.

DEFENDING & NURTURING
THE INNOCENCE & WONDER OF CHILDREN

As part of their delight in all forms of Earthly life, elders—whether or not they are grandparents—derive immense joy from observing and interacting with children. Keenly perceiving and appreciating the soul of the Earth, elders are adept at recognizing wild nature in human children, in particular their natural innocence and wonder, essential foundations for all that follows in life. Elders defend these qualities in children from whatever elements of their society might compromise child-nature.

But elders do more than defend these qualities; they also directly nurture them through their interactions with children and through promoting whole-child-development practices and curricula that emphasize immersion in the other-than-human world as much as in human culture. For example, elders advocate and model the importance in early childhood of touch, play, stories, and time outside with other-than-human nature. For older children, they champion, for instance, the need for free play in undomesticated environments, the celebration of the imagination and senses, the thorough exploration and embrace of emotions, and the enjoyment of sacred stories (mythology and cosmology).[8]

Earth elder Thomas Berry regularly reminded us that children must understand that their home is not the industrial world but the world of "woodlands and meadows and flowers and birds and mountains and valleys and streams and stars."[9] Thomas counseled us that children must also be enabled to directly experience the Universe. In fact, he believed the child is our guide to how the Universe ought to be experienced by *all* of us.

Caring for the soul of children is one of the keystones of responding, in both a practical and spiritual way, to our current ecological crises.

MENTORING & INITIATING ADOLESCENTS

In the role of mentor, elders tutor adolescent youth in human development, teaching about life stages and passages, tasks and archetypes, subpersonalities, human wholeness, and psychological types. Elders help adolescents appreciate their own developing uniqueness and wholeness. They support youth in finding their way through the maze of teenage challenges—through value exploration, for example, and emotional access and expression, relationship with the inner critic, and the minefields of authenticity, personal conflicts, and sex.

Even more vitally, it's the elders who have the knack to recognize when particular youths are ready to enter their time of initiatory instruction and of wandering into the realms of soul—a kind of wandering that is at once psychological, spiritual, geographical, and cultural. Elders play a central role in instructing and initiating youths, helping them disengage from their early-adolescent identities, teaching them soul-encounter skills and practices, and preparing them to assume their unique roles in the community and, more generally, on Earth.[10]

The elder's ecocentric outlook informs them that, if their culture is going to remain vital and continue to evolve, the adolescents must be initiated into their individual destinies. Elders appreciate the big picture of human development and see the deeper significance of the social and psychospiritual struggles of youth.

GUIDING THE EVOLUTION
OR TRANSFORMATION OF CULTURE

A third dimension of caring for the soul of the world is to oversee, individually and collectively, the evolving direction of the culture. Technical advancements, environmental changes, and social and cultural shifts can require significant modifications in the organization, agenda, or values of society. With the multidimensional global crisis of our time, this is especially true, perhaps more than ever in the human story. We are in great need of true elders to guide us through the terribly difficult times to come, to see the need for specific cultural corrections, to design the appropriate responses, and to oversee their implementation. And the true elders need the support of the elder within each one of us and of the cultural eldering function of ecocentric organizations.

An elder is a holder of cultural tradition, but the elder holds not so much the surface forms of the tradition (the specific ways things have been done) as, more importantly, its deep-structural essence, its mythopoetic function, from which depths new forms might emerge to serve cultural evolution.

One of the ways that elder Joanna Macy is influencing the evolving direction of our culture revolves around what she calls "deep time work." This is a collection of perspectives and exercises that help people experience their present lives within much larger temporal contexts, nourishing a strong, felt connection with both past and future generations. The experience of deep time utterly contrasts with the sense of time unique to—and all too prevalent in—contemporary society. "[Our] economy and technologies depend upon decisions made at lightning speed for short-term goals, cutting us off from nature's rhythms and from the past and future as well. Marooned in the present, we are progressively blinded to the sheer ongoingness of time. Both the company of our ancestors and the claims of our descendants become less and less real to us."[11]

In her work with deep time, Joanna invites into our awareness both our forebears and the future beings, to help us comprehend, from a suitably vast perspective—an elder perspective—the choices we must make in this century. Joanna explains that the ultimate purpose of deep-time work is to "save life." Saving life—the life of all species—is a central goal for the elders as she, he, they, we, guide the evolution of the culture.

Another component of Joanna's culture-guiding work is to reassure people that they can openly face the horrors of our current global situation and be empowered by the consequent grief, despair, and strategic challenges.

Elders know that personal maturation often begins with a dying, a positive disintegration, always a necessity before a rebirth. Likewise, elders know that the transformation of contemporary culture, which they are charged to oversee, requires something like a collective descent into our inescapable grief and despair over the real possibility of our self-inflicted extinction, a descent that empowers our will to act and our capacity to respond imaginatively and effectively. The elders of our time must assume the role of underworld guides for the human collective in our current planetary rite of passage. Doing so is caring for the soul of the world.

MAINTAINING THE BALANCE BETWEEN HUMAN CULTURE & THE LARGER EARTH COMMUNITY

This fourth way to care for the soul of the world is perhaps the most vital component of the elder's guardianship of the *anima mundi*. The true elder must take his place as one of the trustees of the culture. This is equally true for the elder within each of us and for those organizations that embody the cultural eldering function. The elders' charge includes the long-term sustainability of the interface between the human and the wild and consequently of the vitality of the land, waters, and air. Elders are defenders of the diversity and integrity of all life.

"Defender of life" is an accurate characterization of Thomas Berry during his elderhood. On his own initiative, as well as in collaboration with many organizations and groups around the world, Thomas led the way in expressing the urgency of refashioning all human affairs to conform to the larger functioning of our planet. He told us that elders must now help the younger generations reinvent culture in all four of its "great establishments that control our lives—the government/legal establishment, the economic/corporation establishment, the education/university establishment, the religious/church or synagogue or mosque establishment."[12]

The core themes of the elder's most vital work are eloquently expressed in the Earth Charter (2000), a worldwide, cross-cultural people's treaty, a Declaration of Interdependence embodying the hopes and aspirations of the emerging global society. From the Earth Charter:

> We stand at a critical moment in Earth's history, a time when humanity must choose its future. As the world becomes increasingly interdependent and fragile, the future at once holds great peril and promise. To move forward we must recognize that in the midst of a magnificent diversity of cultures and life forms we are one human family and one Earth community with a common destiny. We must join together to bring forth a sustainable global society founded on respect for nature, universal human rights, economic justice, and a culture of peace. Towards this end, it is imperative that we, the peoples of the Earth, declare our responsibility to one another, to the greater community of life, and to future generations.[13]

The Earth Charter is one of our finest examples of the cultural eldering function as carried out by a nongovernmental organization.

In an ecocentric and soulcentric society, true elders are the only people eligible to serve as politicians, community leaders, and judges. This is what we find in Lao-tzu's Taoism (from sixth-century BCE China)—the leader or ruler as a person of considerable wisdom and selflessness, qualities that emerge only after decades of soul-infused maturation. A true politician's job is not so much to rule the human community; it is more to oversee the balance or interface between the human realm and the rest of creation, between the village and the greater Earth community. This is a holistic approach to governance in which the foremost principle is right-relationship with the whole, as found, for example, in the traditions of the Haudenosaunee Nation (Iroquois), from whom the eighteenth-century founders of the United States learned and adopted many of the principles of Western democracy.

The history of politics in Western civilization is replete with stories of patho-adolescent power grabbers or, at best, well-intentioned but psychologically adolescent leaders. Genuinely adult politicians are rare; truly *elder* statesmen are even more so. Currently, among the "developed" nations, the United States is leading the way in patho-adolescent politics, in which too many leadership choices are motivated by greed and fear and enabled by immaturity, paranoia, and lack of moral development. With a majority of the electorate being psychologically adolescent themselves, these politicians, despite their records, continue to get elected.

Social and ecological health, therefore, depends on the personal development of all voters, in fact of all people—of all races, ages, genders, and classes—and on the establishment of cultural forms and practices that allow for equitable and genuine human maturation. Elders are the ones most qualified for overseeing this essential project of enhancing individual and collective maturation, which is, in turn, critical for maintaining the balance between human culture and the larger Earth community.

CARING FOR THE SOUL OF THE WORLD
IN AN EGOCENTRIC WORLD

Caring for the soul of the world is difficult even in a healthy culture. But it's particularly challenging in egocentric societies, especially those in the terminal stages of cultural decline.

A much-diminished cadre of elders must now oversee the most extensive and urgent Earth-care in human history.

The current state of the world evokes great anguish and despair for anyone paying attention, but this is especially true for those with mature hearts, who feel the world's degradation all the more acutely. We must learn to behold and hold all this dying and loss, including our own, and still act to preserve and protect what we can.

In our efforts to preserve life and diversity in an egocentric world, our mature anger—in addition to our love—can be one of our greatest resources. Mature anger is part of a healthy reaction to the actions of people in power that cause suffering, death, and extinction for so many individuals, species, and human traditions and languages. This includes anger at ourselves for our complicity, in either minor or major ways. Anger of this kind promotes clarity and motivates constructive and corrective action, as well as compassion for those who are suffering. Mature anger—entirely distinct from hatred—derives, as Tibetan Buddhists say, "straight from the heart of pure compassion."[14]

Caring for the soul of the world today is daunting. We have never been in greater need of true elders, of the eldering function of society's healthiest organizations and institutions, and of the elder dimension within every human psyche. The *anima mundi* depends on it.

*God redeems humanity, but nature needs to be redeemed
by human alchemists, who are able to induce the process of
transformation, which alone is capable of liberating
the light imprisoned in physical creation.*

STEPHAN HOELLER

SANDRA INGERMAN *works with the ancient practice of shamanism to heal the Earth and ourselves. Recognizing that the world is dangerously out of balance, she sees this as a time to fully embody Earth wisdom and apply the spiritually transformative power of shamanism. If we work together, the energy of our spiritual collective can transform the planet.*

Medicine for the Earth
SANDRA INGERMAN

I FEEL VERY HOPEFUL that we will come through the ecological crisis we are now facing. I feel hopeful about the future. And the reason for my hope is that I have witnessed the power of the ancient spiritual practice of shamanism to heal and transform alongside other spiritual traditions.

It is time for us to apply the spiritual forms of healing to the ecological crisis of our times, while embracing shamanism as a way of life. In order to have long-term healing, we must live a life that honors and respects the earth and all of life.

Shamans and spiritual healers look through the eyes of spirit into a client's body, reading its field of energy. Shamans heal what is out of balance on a spiritual level. The illness might manifest on an emotional or physical level, but the shaman looks behind the manifestation of symptoms into the ordinarily hidden energy system of a client to restore harmony on a spiritual level. Once harmony is restored in the invisible energetic system, the client's body and emotions can heal. This is no less true when we look at the level of illness manifesting on the earth in our current ecological crisis.

In the modern Western world our tendency is to try to cure symptoms. We often overlook the core energetic system and how that needs to be restored to a state of balance so that the entire life force of a person and the planet can flow again toward a state of well-being.

205

To truly create positive healing for the planet, as well as for ourselves and others, we must stop focusing on symptoms. We must look through the eyes of spirit to see the movement of energy and any blocks that might be discovered in the energetic web of life.

Indigenous teachings embrace the divine feminine in a way that is crucial for healing the earth and ourselves. For thousands of years it has been known that everything that exists in this world is alive and has a spirit. We are connected to a web of life that reflects the impact of the behavior of all that is alive. We can speak to the spirit of the trees, plants, rocks, rivers, animals, birds, insects, and reptiles and perceive their divine nature. As everything that exists is alive, each being also recognizes the divine in us. The earth is alive and is a sacred being. It is time for us to align with the heartbeat of the earth.

In shamanism we find a practice that comes from various traditions called deep listening. The answers we seek lie in nature—nature is always sharing her teachings with us. The answers also lie in our own inner wisdom. We must shift the focus of our energy from our heads to our hearts, where we can listen to this wisdom. We must remember what we love about life and what brings us to a place of awe and wonder, reigniting our passion. We must remember how to honor and respect life with each breath, step, word, and thought. What you bless blesses you in return. This is the power of reciprocity.

We can use the practice of deep listening to go beyond what our ordinary ears can hear, reaching the divine voice that speaks of the loving feminine wisdom that connects us all. To be of ultimate service to the planet we must reconnect to the divine feminine that teaches us the power of change that comes from being, as opposed to doing.

In the Western world we tend to search out rational solutions for the challenges we face. We attempt to come up with a plan. The ecological issues we are facing need more than a rational plan of action. We must call in and surrender to the power of Spirit, the Divine, Source, God, the Goddess to open the doorway for true healing to occur. We must surrender to the power of love.

PRINCIPLES OF MEDICINE FOR THE EARTH

Through my studies of shamanism I learned to bridge ancient spiritual healing methods and modern day Western culture. One major focus of that for me has been on looking at how ancient spiritual methods could reverse environmental pollution.

As I worked with my own helping spirits, I started to be shown certain basic principles that went into the spiritual work required to turn our ecological crisis around. The work I learned through practicing shamanism also crossed over into spiritual teachings that come from esoteric Christianity, the Kabbalah, and various alchemical, Taoist, Hindu, yogic, and ancient Egyptian works.

The outer world that we live in is a reflection of our inner state of consciousness. This is seen in the teaching "as above, so below; as within, so without." This means that from a spiritual perspective the toxicity we see in our environment is a reflection of our own inner toxicity.

In shamanism it is understood that thoughts are substantial things. It is also understood that words are seeds. In its original Aramaic, the term *abracadabra* is *"abraq ad habra,"* which is literally translated as, "I will create as I speak."

In indigenous cultures the difference between expressing problematic thoughts or emotions and sending them is well understood. In our Western culture, where we do not validate what is happening in the energetic and invisible realms, we often find ourselves filled with toxic thoughts and emotions that we then send out into the world. Without realizing it we can end up sending "poisonous energies" to others, the planet, and even back upon ourselves.

The key is to learn how to acknowledge the depth of our feelings that we all have. We must acknowledge them and then transform the energy behind our thoughts and words.

We need to learn to replace defeatist attitudes and beliefs with thoughts and words that will lead to our desired outcome.

In all spiritual traditions it is taught that everything that manifests in the physical world starts in the invisible realms of spirit.

We must remember that a baby grows in the womb. Trees and plants start with a seed that is nurtured in the earth and then expands into roots, branches, leaves, buds, fruits, and flowers. Creation comes through us.

We often expect change just to happen magically without the inner work that is needed to create outer change. We want science to magically create "a cure" for all the ills of our times. But the true changes we are looking for must come from within. We need to incorporate spiritual practices into our daily lives and live the practices.

We need to be able to work through the dark states of consciousness and transform them into golden light. This is the true meaning of alchemy. And then our outer world will reflect our state of light back to us.

We must remember that we are not just form and matter. We are luminous beings. And our destiny is to radiate light.

Right now many of us walk around with unexamined thoughts, attitudes, and emotions. We live a life filled with fear and this generates states of hate and war. We believe that there is scarcity of resources and that we are limited in what we can create. This is a reflection of how we live from a place of separation.

When we tap into our divine and luminous nature we once again move into a place of oneness. And in a state of oneness we experience only love and abundance. All healing and creation become possible.

At the same time we must remember that in oneness we are connected to all of life on this earth, joined together in a web of life. This means we must live from a place of honor and respect. We are part of nature, not separate from it. The elements are alive—earth, air, water, and fire (both as the sun and the fire at the earth's core) give us life. Realizing this, we will never pollute that which gives us life.

The ultimate teaching is, "It is who we become that changes the world and not what we do." The part of us that is "becoming" involves remembering that we are spiritual beings whose destiny is to radiate light and channel unconditional love. We came here to learn about the power of love and to create from love. The part that we are "doing" involves how we walk on this earth as conscious beings. We must be conscious of every action, thought, and word. For once again, our outer world is a reflection of our inner state.

Our perception creates our reality. We must learn how to shift our perception about what is going on in our lives and on the planet. We must embrace a consciousness where we perceive beauty and abundance. And we do this by being grateful for all that life brings to us and for us.

I researched different traditions to find clues how miracles were performed by shamans, mystics, and saints. As I read, a formula that seemed to be part of all miracles started to emerge. Each element of the formula could not be taken separately, but when combined, they created the transmutation or "miracle." In this context, transmutation can be understood as the ability to change the nature of a substance; in our particular context, this could mean that the work of effecting environmental change is to change toxic substances into neutral or harmless substances.

Eventually I stated the formula as *intention + union + love + harmony + concentration + focus + imagination = transmutation.* For miracles to occur, we must hold a strong intention of what we want to see happen. All spiritual practices teach about the power of intention, which inevitably leads to action.

Furthermore, miracles involve union with a divine force, which is the source of love. Love is a great transformer and an essential ingredient in all miracles. Where there is an open heart filled with love, miraculous energy may be brought out into life. Being in the presence of people who imbue the power of love can produce healing in and of itself. These people often do not use methods or techniques; their mere presence lifts up everyone around them into a higher consciousness.

Spiritual traditions also teach that to be healthy we must live a harmonious life. Harmony within creates harmony without. Most tell us, too, that a key to the success of a spiritual practice is the ability to concentrate on the work we are doing. At the same time we must maintain a strong focus on both our short-term and our long-term goals.

Imagination is another key element in performing the miracle of transmutation. We must be able to envision an environment that is pure and clean and which supports all of life. With the power of imagination, we have the ability to sculpt the world we live in.

Many shamans say we are dreaming the wrong dream. We live with the illusion that we are separate from nature, separate from the spiritual realms, and that we are victims of our life and our environment. These illusions are seeds that grow into plants of fear, anger, hate, despair, and darkness. We need a new dream to create a new earth.

In 1997 I had a powerful dream in which the Egyptian god Anubis appeared to me and told me that the key to the work of reversing environmental pollution is transfiguration. I had heard stories from shamanic traditions about shamans shapeshifting into animals such as wolves and ravens. But I could not at first connect that practice to that of reversing environmental pollution.

An important insight about this came from one of my clients who was dying of cancer. When I told her about my dream, she became very animated and started to share her passion for stories about Jesus. Being a fundamentalist Christian, she knew quite well how Jesus transfigured, where he began to shine with bright rays of light. While in this transfigured state of divine light he worked miraculous healings.

Now I understood Anubis' message to me: light heals and transmutes. And my research into various spiritual books showed countless references to healers and spiritual masters transfiguring into divine light when performing miraculous healings. Since we are essentially spiritual light connected to all beings, spirit is who we are beyond our skin. When we drop all that separates us from our divine light, everything around us is mirrored back as a state of divinity, light, and perfection.

For years I worked with groups of people on an experiment to see if as a community we could transmute pollution in the environment from toxicity to a neutral substance. We took de-ionized (pure) water and polluted it with ammonium hydroxide, which is a common pollutant in the environment, and is a strong base. It is easy to check its presence with the use of pH strips that measure alkalinity. Our ceremony involved letting go of what keeps us separate from our own divinity, and feeling ourselves as the power of the universe, the divine source of light and universal love. The water reflects back to us that place of complete harmony, and in that place, we radiate spiritual light that affects everything around us. I have presented this work to many groups, and every time the pH of the water has dropped 1–3 points toward neutral. From a scientific point of view this would be seen as impossible.

Since these initial experiments, I started using a gas discharge visualization (GDV) camera that allows one to capture the physical, emotional, mental, and spiritual energies emanating from a person, plant, liquid, powder, or inanimate object and translate those energies into a computerized model. In other words, this diagnostic camera measures and evaluates the energy of the auric field and integrates that information into a computer-generated report with pictures. The camera enabled us to document the change in energy of the substances present in our circle. To change the variables in the experiment, we also put food (a peach and crackers) and soil in our circle, along with the water, and the GDV camera was able to capture the positive change of energy of those items as well as the water.

When working in this way, we perceive everyone and everything in the room in its divinity. Although on a physical level there might be reports of illness, on a spiritual level we recognize the divine perfection of all of life. In this way we stimulate the radiance of each being to shine forth. As we begin to change our consciousness and get in touch with the light inside us, we can effect great changes in our outer world. It is who we *become* that changes the world.

WE ARE THE DREAMERS OF A NEW DREAM

As I wrote earlier, shamans around the world believe that we are dreaming the wrong dream. For everything that occurs in life is a dream. Inasmuch as we have forgotten this teaching in the West, we end up focusing our thoughts and our imaginations on feeding the problems and challenges in the world. We must practice using our imagination to dream the dream of the earth, that we embrace love, peace, light, abundance, equality for all.

The fabric of reality is breaking down. Floods, hurricanes, tornadoes, earthquakes are unweaving the fabric of life. Organizational structures are falling apart, resulting in vast disillusionment with government and religious organizations.

We are continuing to experience major earth changes. And this is part of evolution. Today land extends over what was once water, and water covers what was once land. The earth continues to evolve and change just as human consciousness is evolving.

Together we are going through an initiation. Initiations mark a change. And all change involves a death. Death is not an end; it is a transition to something new. We are moving towards a new and healthier way of life. And this means we must let go of the old paradigms that no longer support all of life in a healthy way. At the same time, as we let go of the old, we must hold a positive attitude and vision for the new dream that is unfolding.

True shamans work on creating the new fabric of reality and continue to work on the web of life. Looking at patterns of disharmony, they use art, song, dance, and dreaming to change the frequency of the patterns of the entire web.

To change the collective fabric requires changing our thoughts and daydreams. As we work to create a new fabric of reality in the invisible realms, it will manifest into the physical world to replace all that is unraveling. In this way we build an invisible world of substance that manifests as a new physical reality.

When we use our thoughts, words, and daydreams to build an invisible world of substance, we go to the core of reweaving a new fabric reality.

If people do not come forth who are willing to be the dreamers, then what will our future be? As evolutionary breakdowns will keep occurring regardless of our involvement in them, what might our vision for their future unfolding be? If we collectively hold a new vision for the future, we discover the power to shape these changes positively.

To do this we must be able to imagine the world we wish to live in. We do this by engaging all our senses of seeing, hearing, feeling, smelling, and tasting. For we must be able to fully imagine living in a world that embraces love, light, harmony, beauty, peace, abundance, and equality for all.

Imagine what it would be like if people around the world joined together to focus their imagination in a way that created a return to a harmonious way of life.

As people feel worn down by life, we move into a place where our senses become increasingly deadened. The media provide images for us instead of allowing beautiful and vivid new images to arise from inside us. We listen to music on MP3 players and iPods, but we do not allow our inner music to play through us.

The key to using our creative imagination is to engage our strong inner senses to produce our own vivid images, sounds, smells, tastes, and feelings. We need to create our own movies with each of us living powerfully in the movie instead of simply passively watching the movie. And we need to fuel our senses with intense enthusiasm. We need to stop allowing the outside world to write our script, and our new script must be born from our inner world. For this, we must use the depth of our senses to make our creations real.

I think that people operate as flat-screen TVs. Where is the depth of our own senses? We are fed so much from the outer world. We need to allow our senses to bubble up from within us, and into the world.

If we cannot get in touch with the true power of our own vivid images, our own internal songs of creation, the beauty of the fragrances we wish to smell, the taste of healthy food grown and cooked with love, and the feeling of touching the beauty of life, all the power of our creation goes out. If our creation is not fueled by passion and enthusiasm in what we project into the world, it loses all force. And the world molds its superficiality back into our creative work, making it lack depth and power.

It is important to keep up our spiritual work to hold a good vision no matter what we see happening in the world. Our dreams replace the unraveling fabric of the world and create a new healthy fabric of reality.

Often people say to me that the future is much greater than we can imagine. Then they ask me what will happen if they imagine the future based on what their ego wishes for, fearing this might not be imagined from their highest spiritual consciousness. My answer to this is to simply explain that we are using our imagination twenty-four hours a day, seven days a week. We all use our imaginations constantly, though sadly it is often not in a mindful manner. But once we set our intention to create a good outcome, the spiritual forces from within and without take over to manifest what is for the best of all concerned. We just need to always open our hearts in love for all of life when we do our dreaming. Then the work becomes to surrender the ego to the outcome of our dreams, having intended to create the most positive ones imaginable.

WORKING TOGETHER AS A GLOBAL COMMUNITY

In all spiritual traditions we can find examples of the collective power that is generated by a group focusing on healing in contrast to what a single person can do on his or her own.

During one of my Medicine for the Earth trainings, I brought in a peach from a tree growing in my garden. At the time, Santa Fe was in the midst of a terrible drought. I had been doing my spiritual work each day to perceive the trees in their divine light instead of projecting suffering upon them, thereby just feeding the struggle.

When we took a photo of a piece of the peach under the GDV camera it appeared very healthy and vital. But the light and energy field of this peach rose exponentially in the middle of a circle where fifty people were gathered to perceive it in its divine light.

There are countless stories of miraculous healings that have happened to individuals and to the environment when a group focuses together.

One example of this is how plant life grew back in the Gulf of Mexico much faster than anyone had expected after the devastating oil spill in 2010. Millions of people around the world performed spiritual ceremonies and healing work in their own way to bring this about.

We must examine how we work interactively with the global spiritual collective. Millions of people around the world are now engaged in spiritual work. We all work in the ways we are called to, but the work is for the benefit of all of life.

Most of us think about the spiritual collective rationally. But what is truly important is to *feel* the power of the spiritual collective in our body. This is a force. As such, it is both a masculine and feminine principle, approached both by rational thought and embodied feeling.

Right now we feel in our bodies mainly the powerful force of the dense collective mass that believes in scarcity, pollution, and illness, convinced that creating positive change on the planet is impossible. As a consequence, this is the force that keeps being fueled and keeps manifesting its presence through such unrelenting reinforcement.

As we allow ourselves to feel the pure energetic force of the spiritual collective, this power will override the collective trance we are trying to break out of.

The energy and power of the collective builds, and in its state of beingness, it creates a field of energy that transforms; without triggering action in itself, it empowers those in harmony with it to take effective action.

As we set an intention to experience the power of our divine nature and radiate light throughout the planet, we become a vessel for universal love, and as we live a spiritual life, we restore harmony. We must dream together with concentration and focus. We will be successful in creating healing for the planet.

The Creator created the earth and life out of universal love. As the creator, it is time for us to love the earth and all of life. With every breath and every step we take on this great earth, let us join our hearts together in love.

With bended knees, with hands outstretched,
I pray to Thee, my Lord,
Oh Invisible Benevolent Spirit!
Vouchsafe to me in this house of joy,
All righteousness of action, all wisdom of the Good Mind,
That I may therefore bring joy to the Soul of Creation.

THE DIVINE SONGS OF ZOROASTER

Sufi teacher and scholar Pir Zia Inayat Khan *recon-nects us with the sacred traditions of Persia and India that recognize our existence within a spiritually illuminated living universe. The inner world of light and its angelic forces are present throughout creation.*

Persian & Indian Visions
of the Living Earth
Pir Zia Inayat Khan

FROM THE CASPIAN SEA in the west to the Bay of Bengal in the east stretches a vast and undulating tract of the planetary crust marked by soaring peaks, scorched deserts, and fertile river valleys. In the Bronze Age, a migratory people known as the Arya swept into this expanse from the north, establishing the sibling civilizations of Aryana-Vaejah (Iran) and Bharata (India). In Iran arose Mazdaism; India gave rise to Hinduism, Jainism, and Buddhism. In the seventh century CE, Islam appeared in Arabia and began to spread eastward. By the High Middle Ages, the land of the Aryas was also the land of Islam.

Ideas do not occur in a vacuum, and spiritual ideas are no exception. Sacred visions emerge from the disposition of human personalities, from the shape of historical events, and from the momentum of hallowed customs, but perhaps most fundamentally (transcendental sources aside), they emerge from "airs, waters, and places," from the character of the landscapes in which they are born.

When epiphanies are redacted and passed down, the loamy pungency of their genesis frequently fades away, so that an abstract doctrine is perpetuated in place of an embodied insight. Such, however, is not always the case. Spiritual traditions are often the deepest repositories of a culture's knowledge of the ancient bond between person and planet, soul and soil. This is abundantly illustrated in the traditions of Hinduism, Zoroastrianism, and Islam—traditions that, as we shall see, are sometimes intertwined.

Little is known about the outer life of Zoroaster, the great Iranian prophet who lived perhaps a thousand years before Christ. The absence of hard historical facts concerning his life, death, and mission is compensated, however, by the revelatory power of his Avestan songs, the Gathas, and the traditions that have come down concerning his inner life. These songs and traditions paint the portrait of an illuminated mind deeply absorbed in contemplation of the sacred order of the cosmos and alive to its profoundest mysteries.

An account of Zoroaster's discovery of his prophetic vocation is given in the Pahlavi book, *Selections of Zad-Sparam*. The book relates that in his thirtieth year, while taking part in the annual festival of spring, Zoroaster waded in the river Daiti. Four times, at four different depths—the last so deep that only his head remained dry—he forded the river. As he emerged, an enormous figure garbed in light approached him. It was Vohu Mana, the Good Mind. Bidding Zoroaster follow, Vohu Mana ushered him to an assembly of pure spirits, where Ahura Mazda (Lord Wisdom) presided, attended by his seven Powers. Zoroaster inquired of Mazda concerning perfection, and received the answer that the first perfection is good thought; the second, good speech; and the third, good action.

Over the years that followed, Zoroaster was admitted to six further conferences. Ahura Mazda no longer appeared; his Powers, the Holy Immortals, now bestowed their blessings on the prophet, each in turn.

Zoroaster held audience with Vohu Mana, the protector of the animal kingdom, on the twin peaks of Hukairya and Ausind, the "two holy communing ones," linked by a cataract of primordial waters. Bearing witness were representatives of the five types of animal: swimming, burrowing, flying, ranging, and grazing. The assembled animals confessed their faith in the religion of Ahura Mazda, and Vohu Mana conferred on Zoroaster the custodianship of the animal kingdom.

Arta Vahishta (Perfect Existence), the governor of fire in all of its forms, appeared to the prophet at "the Tojan water"—probably the Tejen river in Turkmenistan. Amidst a throng of fire elementals, Arta Vahishta instructed Zoroaster in the maintenance of holy fires.

Kshatra Vairya (Desirable Reign), the patron of metals, next showed himself amidst a congregation of metal spirits. His instructions concerned the preservation and proper use of various metals.

Now came, in succession, the feminine Immortals. The first of these was Spenta Armaiti (Holy Devotion), whose province is the Earth. Spenta Armaiti received Zoroaster beside a spring on the slope of Mount Asnavad, surrounded by a retinue of telluric spirits associated with a range of "regions, frontiers, stations, settlements, and districts."[1] Into the prophet's charge she placed the care of the Earth.

On the same mountain, Zoroaster beheld a vision of Harvetat (Integrity), the tutelary Archangel of waters. Spirits of rivers and seas attended him as he received the Immortal's benediction and instruction in the guardianship and propitiation of water.

Finally, on the bank of the Daiti River, surrounded by a company of plant spirits, the prophet was admitted to an audience with Amertat (Immortality), the preserver of the vegetal kingdom. She duly taught him how to care for and propitiate plants.

Zoroaster's prophetic message, enshrined in the Avesta, represents a chivalric call to arms in defense of the holy order of creation against the forces of evil, darkness, and pollution personified by Angra Mainyu (Destructive Mind) and his diabolical horde. As Ahura Mazda has his six Holy Immortals, six Archfiends are sworn to Angra Mainyu's service. These are, in the Pahlavi tongue: Akoman, the evil genius; Andar, the tempter; Savar, the agent of misgovernment; Naikiyas, the fomenter of discontent; Taprev, the poisoner of plants and animals; and Zairik, the manufacturer of poisons.

Compromise with these malefactors is unthinkable. The worshipper of Mazda must purify himself and the world of their stain by the scrupulous practice of good thought, good speech, and good action. The forces of light will thus gain ground, advancing in ascendancy, dispelling malevolence, and speeding the long-awaited day known as the *frashkart*, when the whole of creation is to be purified, redeemed, illuminated, and rendered immortal.

The Zoroastrian faith flourished under the Achaemenid, Seleucid, Parthian, and Sassanian dynasties, which successively held sway for over a thousand years. The fall of the Sassanian Empire in the seventh century CE spelled the decline of the faith. By the end of the eleventh century, Islam had become the new language of the sacred, and only a minute number of Iranians still adhered to the creed of Zoroaster.

Still, many of the old motifs lived on. The Persians kept their solar calendar and continued to observe the festivals of the New Year and spring. Zoroaster was commonly remembered as an ancient prophet, and the poet Firdawsi (d. 1020) preserved the legends of the pre-Islamic heroes and sages in his celebrated epic, the *Shahnama*. Nor was Zoroaster's vision of the living Earth forgotten, for the angelology of the old faith was revived by the Sufi philosopher Shahab al-Din Yahya Suhrawardi (d. 1191).

Suhrawardi saw himself as the heir of a wisdom tradition originating with the antediluvian Egyptian prophet-king Hermes Trismegistus. According to the philosopher's account, Hermes' legacy migrated to Greece, where the pre-Socratics and Platonists were its custodians, and to Persia, where it was kept alive by a succession of enlightened kings and priests, including the prophet Zoroaster. Suhrawardi held that certain Sufi saints introduced these kindred traditions into the civilization of Islam, and that he was their reunifier.

Suhrawardi's unification of Neoplatonism and Mazdaism finds expression in the conception of an animate universe teeming with angelic lights. All that exists is of light, for light is existence itself, the very essence of apparency. God is the "Light of Lights," and as light kindles light, creation proliferates as a cascade of illumination poured into the dark abyss of non-being. In this great chain of being, the angels are links, uniting the manifest world with the infinite brilliance that is its source.

Suhrawardi's angelic hierarchy consists of three orders, named respectively the "Mothers," the "Lords of the Species," and the "Regent Lights." The Mothers are a vertical order descending in procession, one after another, by the principle of emanation. The first of this line is Bahman, the Avestan Immortal Vohu Mana. There follows a long, though not infinite, series of Intellects, each receiving light from the Light of Lights and its predecessors, and bequeathing light to its successors. By this causal chain the starry sky is lit up.

The Lords of the Species are a horizontal order brought into being by the Mothers. Here are found the archetypes of the kingdoms of creation that compose the natural world. Nothing exists on Earth without an underpinning in the world of pure light. Amongst the Lords of the Species are the remaining five Immortals of Mazdaism: Arta Vahishta, Kshatra Vairya, Spenta Armaiti, Harvetat, and Amertat, who spiritually epitomize fire, metals, the Earth, water, and plants. The angelic archetype of the human race is Gabriel.

The third order of Suhrawardi's angelic hierarchy, the Regent Lights, is a subsidiary of the second order. Whereas the Lords of the Species are the archetypes of the various classes of created beings, the Regent Lights are the forces that animate and govern these beings. Among the Regent Lights are angels who move the spheres, angels who govern human lives, and angels who watch over animals, minerals, and plants.

These Regent Lights correspond to the *fravashis* of Mazdaism, which are the spiritual essences of every existing person and thing. The Mazdean hymn dedicated to the *fravashis*, entitled Farvardin Yasht, is an invocation of generous compass, calling blessings upon the beneficent face of creation in all of its human and non-human manifestations, past, present, and future. The priestly author proclaims: "We worship this Earth; We worship those heavens; We worship those good things that stand between and that are worthy of sacrifice and prayer and are to be worshipped by the faithful man. We worship the souls of the wild beasts and of the tame. We worship the souls of the holy men and women, born at any time, whose consciences struggle, or will struggle, or have struggled, for the good."[2]

In like fashion, Suhrawardi's cosmology envisions a universe that is intensely alive and inherently sacred. All existence is the effusion, in pulsing waves, of the holy of holies, the Light of Lights. Transpiring in every clod, puddle, flaming wick, and fluttering breeze is an angelic presence, a sentient and radiant delegate of the cosmic order.

For all his interest in the wisdom traditions of Greece and Persia, Suhrawardi remained a devoted Muslim. For him, there was no contradiction between the ancient schools of wisdom and the revelation announced by the prophet Muhammad—a revelation that, after all, declares, "Allah is the Light of the heavens and Earth" (24:35).

The Qur'an begins, "Read in the name of your Lord" (96:1). What must be read are the *ayat*, the signs of God. The verses of scripture are signs, but so too are the verses inscribed "on the horizons and in themselves" (41:53). The holy books of the prophets, Earth's rapturous geography, and the interior landscapes of the human soul are all of a piece, all pages in a single book, the book in which God's own story is told. This is a story without end, for, "If all the trees on Earth were pens and the ocean ink, with seven oceans behind it to add to its supply, yet the words of God would not be exhausted" (31:27).

Just as Suhrawardi drew upon Mazdaism to elaborate his Sufism, four centuries later the Mazdean philosopher Azar Kayvan returned the compliment, drawing on Sufism to articulate his Avestan worldview. Azar Kayvan's mystical poems are assembled, with commentary, in the volume *Jam-i Kay Khusraw*. The poems describe the philosopher's journey through the inner and outer kingdoms and spheres in the course of four ascensions, each culminating in a swoon of *unio mystica*, or dissolution in the Absolute. Along the way, Azar Kayvan encounters the angelic Intellects of the seven celestial spheres. Before reaching interplanetary space, however, he must make his way through the realms of the sub-lunar elements. This is how he describes his progress:

A welter of fires I saw, of countless hues
    Invisible but to the gaze of statues.
As these fires now blazed up in great tongues
        of flame
    At once I took wing—sir, a bird I became.
Now I was swimming in seas, rivers, and creeks,
    Now roaming through tenements on cobbled
        streets.
Here a brisk and shimmering conflagration,
    There fresh air, tonic for the constitution.
Ho! Anon what bright waters were glistening
    Then a cityscape—sir, are you listening?[3]

The poet's disciple and commentator explains, "The fire he sees in the beginning signifies traversing the fire in one's self. Flying in the air signifies crossing one's aerial part. Swimming in, and gliding on, oceans and rivers signifies navigating the liquid element of one's body. Moving among streets and walls and houses signifies passing through one's telluric part."[4]

Azar Kayvan emigrated from Iran, where Mazdeans were a beleaguered minority, to India, where the Mughal emperor Akbar had established "universal peace" as the law of the land. At Akbar's court, priests of various religions assembled for theological discussion, and Hindu sacred texts were translated into Persian, the language of Indian Muslims. In fact, the dialogue between Islam and Hinduism had already been underway in India for the last four hundred years, its richest exchanges taking place in the running conversation between the Chishti Sufis and Nathpanthi yogis.

The founder of the Chishti Order, Khwaja Mu'in al-Din Chishti (d. 1230), is traditionally remembered both as a triumphant rival of the yogis, and as a sympathetic student and master of their esoteric lore. To him are attributed a number of treatises devoted to esoteric physiology, the science of the breath, and the mysteries of the four elements.

As widely different as were the theological views of Muslim Sufis and Hindu yogis, they had two spiritual perceptions fully in common: the vital livingness of the elements and the status of the human form as a microcosm encapsulating the breadth, depth, and range of the whole universe.

The livingness of the elements is attested in the sacred texts of Islam. The Qur'an invokes earth, water, and fire as signs of God's power and benevolence. "And the earth shall shine with the light of its Lord" (39:69). "Of water [We] fashioned every living being" (21:30). "[He] has made for you, out of a green tree, fire" (36:80). Concerning air, a *hadith*, or prophetic tradition, says, "Do not curse the wind, for it derives from the breath of the All-Merciful." From a position steeped in the Qur'anic revelation, the poet Rumi wrote, "Air, earth, water, and fire are God's servants. To us they seem lifeless, but to God living."[5]

The Hindu tradition is no less emphatic in its veneration of the sacred order of the cosmos. The Atharva Veda invokes earth as a holy mother. The Indian rivers Ganges, Yamuna, Narmada, and Kaveri are living symbols of the highest spiritual purity. Fire is personified in the Vedas in the divine figure of Agni, and air in the figure of Vayu. All four of the elements—together with the fifth, space—are bounteous channels of grace, purification, and benediction. The Vamana Purana sings, "Let all the great elements bless the dawning day: Earth with its smell, water with its taste, fire with its radiance, air with its touch, and sky with its sound."[6]

Hindu acts of worship are traditionally preceded by *bhutashuddhi*, the ritual purification of the elements in the body and in the landscape. In this manner the inner and outer dimensions of the universe are brought into symmetry, and the human being is sanctified as an epitome of the surrounding totality. The human heart contains fire and air, sun and moon, lightning and stars, pronounces the Chandogya Upanishad.

The Chishti Sufis share this perception. In the *Sum of Yoga* attributed to Khwaja Mu'in al-Din Chishti, the entire cosmos is mapped onto the human form:

> Know that by His power God Most High created
> the human body to contain all that He created in
> the universe: "We will show them Our signs in
> the horizons and in themselves, until they see ..."
> (41:53). God created the twelve signs of the zodiac
> in the heavens and also in the human body. The

head is Aries, the neck is Taurus, the hands are Gemini, the arms are Cancer, the chest is Leo, the intestine is Virgo, the navel is Libra, the phallus is Scorpio, the thighs are Sagittarius, the knees are Capricorn, the shanks are Aquarius, the soles of the feet are Pisces. The seven planets that revolve beneath the zodiac may be located thus: the heart is the Sun, the liver is Jupiter, the pulmonary artery is the Moon, the kidneys are Venus, the spleen is Saturn, the brain is Mercury, the gall bladder is Mars. God the Glorious and Most High made 360 days in the year, 360 revolutions in the zodiac, 360 mountains on the face of the Earth, 360 great rivers, and in the human body, 360 segments of bone (like the mountains), 360 arteries (like the rivers), 360 epidermal tissues (like the days of the year). The motion of the stomach is like the sea, hairs are like trees, parasites are like beasts of the jungle, the face is like a built-up city, and the skin is like the desert. The world has its four seasons, and these are also present in man: infancy is spring, youth is summer, quiescence is fall, and old age is winter. Thunder corresponds to the voice, lightning to laughter, rain to tears.[7]

To bring microcosm and macrocosm into harmony, yogis and Sufis practiced, and still today practice, *kriyas*, or meditations, corresponding to the four elements. In his *Secret of Love*, the twentieth-century Chishti Sufi 'Aziz Miyan describes the elemental *kriyas* in this manner: "Earth *kriya*: Meditate while incrementally burying the body in the ground, from feet to head. Water *kriya*: Meditate while sitting underwater, lying in the rain, or pouring water over the body. Fire *kriya*: Meditate before a fire, uniting first with the smoke and then with the flame. Air *kriya*: Meditate standing on a tree, hill, or roof, wearing a single cloth, facing the wind. Breathe in and out slowly and deeply, inducing the sensation of flight."[8]

Another prominent Indian Sufi of the twentieth century, Hazrat Inayat Khan, taught a series of breaths for the purification of the elements in the body and mind. These twenty breaths form a foundational daily practice in the Order he established in London in 1917. Hazrat Inayat Khan conceived of the Earth as an animate, and in some sense sentient, whole. He wrote, "If the planet on which we live had no intelligence it could not have intelligent beings on it."[9] If Earth possesses a kind of sentience, it follows that the planet may be susceptible to suffering, and Hazrat Inayat Khan made just such an assertion when he wrote, "My deep sigh rises above as a cry of the Earth, and an answer comes from within as a message."[10] The message of his talks and writings was a call to contemplate the moral and spiritual interconnectedness, and ultimate ontological unity, of all life.

The theme of the Earth's cry may be traced all the way back to Zoroaster. In the twenty-ninth Yasna of the Gathas, the Earth is represented in the figure of the soul of a cow. The cow lifts up her voice to Ahura Mazda, wailing, "For whom have you brought me into being? Who shaped me? Wrath and rapine, insolence, aggression, and violence sit upon me in my affliction. No one is my protector except you, O God, so reveal to me the good shepherd, the deliverer."[11] Ahura Mazda responds by appointing Zoroaster as Earth's guardian—a response the soul of the cow greets with endearing skepticism.

A similar event occurs in the Bhagavata Purana, a major text of medieval Indian Vaishnavism. In this narrative, the Earth again assumes the form of a cow and tearfully submits her complaint, this time to Brahma, who in turn conveys it to Vishnu. In answer, Vishnu undertakes to incarnate in the form of Krishna to champion Earth's cause.

The sacred texts of Mazdaism, Hinduism, and Islam provide a profusion of illuminating perspectives on the nature of embodied existence. While there are undeniable differences in the worldviews communicated in these texts, certain key principles emerge as common understandings. Foremost among these is the insight that the manifest universe is a marvel of providential grace. Following on this is the perception that not only humans, animals, and plants, but all material forms partake of the pervasive light and power of creation, and bear recognition as spiritually alive. Further, the texts make clear the error of imagining human life as hovering autonomously above the natural world. Mystical contemplation of the human form conduces to the realization that the body is profoundly embedded within the wholeness of nature, a totality that each human physically and spiritually personifies. The Indo-Persian prophetic traditions agree: the Earth is alive, we live in and through her, and as we are in her keeping, so is she in ours.

The world is charged with the grandeur of God.
It will flame out, like shining from shook foil …

GERARD MANLEY HOPKINS

FR. RICHARD ROHR, *a Franciscan monk, passionately reminds us of the Christian teachings that the world is the incarnation of God and the primary divine revelation— that the whole world is the body of God. While the theology he addresses here is specifically Christian, the larger truths and misconceptions he points to are not limited to Christian experience and belief. This essay serves as an eloquent example of the way our modern world in general has distorted or lost the original understanding of the divinity of the world, resulting in our present ecological crisis.*

Creation as the Body of God
RICHARD ROHR

Creation is the primary and most perfect
revelation of the Divine.
—THOMAS AQUINAS

God remains in immediate sustaining
attentiveness to everything that exists,
precisely in its "thisness."
—JOHN DUNS SCOTUS

The following article, originally written for a Christian audience, recognizes that very poor Christian theology has played a big part in allowing the West to move forward with such a tragic notion of physicality, embodiment, sexuality, animal care, and reverence for the earth, despite our supposed belief that the Eternal Word of God became "flesh" (John 1:14).

I am not presuming that all readers would agree with our Christian belief in this incarnation of God in Jesus, but I do need to point out the full implications for Christians themselves, and invite all sincere seekers into what is good and universal (*philosophia perennis*) about this part of the Christian revelation. Forgive my somewhat hard words toward the end of this article; they reflect, I hope, the urgency of love toward my own.

—*Preface*, FR. RICHARD ROHR

THE INCARNATION of God did not happen in Bethlehem two thousand years ago. That is just when some of us started taking it seriously. The incarnation actually happened approximately 14.5 billion years ago with a moment that we now call "The Big Bang." That is when God actually decided to *materialize* and to *expose who God is*. This alone provides any solid basis for reverence, universal sacrality, and our attempts to form a spiritual ecology that transcends groups and religions.

Two thousand years ago marked the *human* incarnation of God in Jesus, we Christians believe, but before that there was the first and original incarnation through light, water, land, sun, moon, stars, plants, trees, fruit, birds, serpents, cattle, fish, and "every kind of wild beast," according to our Judeo-Christian creation story (Genesis 1:3–25). This was the "Cosmic Christ" through which God has "let us know the mystery of his purpose, the hidden plan he so kindly made from the beginning in Christ" (Ephesians 1:9). You see, *Christ* is not Jesus' last name, but the title for his life's purpose. (Some believe, as I do myself, that the ancient Hindu love of *Krishna*, also a human avatar and incarnation of the divine, was revealing the very same mystery.)

Jesus is a concrete truth revealing and standing in for the eternal truth of the union between the divine and the human, or the Christ Mystery—or Krishna. I myself believe this, but just to believe it is not to live it. The living of this *love mystery* is the important thing and not the correct naming of it! I have met Hasidic Jews, Hesychastic Orthodox, Sufi Muslims, and "pagan" animists who live it much better than we do.

As the *Letter to the Colossians* puts it, "He is the image of the invisible God, the first born of all creation" (1:15); he is the one glorious part that names and reveals the even more glorious whole. "The fullness is founded in him, everything in heaven and everything on earth" (1:19–20). Or as our Franciscan philosopher, John Duns Scotus (1266–1308), put it, Christ was "the very first idea in the mind of God," and *God has never stopped thinking, dreaming, and creating the Eternal Christ Mystery.* The Dominican Thomas Aquinas (1225–1274) adds, "The immense diversity and pluriformity of this creation more perfectly represents God than any one creature alone or by itself."

For most of us, this understanding represents a significant shaking of our foundational image of the universe and of our religion, I am sad to say. Many Christians have seen the world as sadly inert, non-enchanted, unholy, and even dangerous and evil. As if God's creation could be separate from God! Yet if any group should have come to this quite simply and naturally, it should have been those three groups of believers that call themselves "monotheists": Jews, Christians, and Muslims all claim to believe that the world was created by *one good* God. It would seem to follow therefore that everything—everything without exception—would bear the clear imprint and likeness of this one Creator. How could we miss that? Did Satan, in fact, create some of us? We monotheists are the very ones who said "No!" to that. We believed that "One God created everything out of nothing" (Genesis 1:2).

We could perhaps say that this terrible misperception was a disastrous act of human self-congratulation and self-absorption. For some reason, Christians thought humans were the only creatures that God cared about, and all else was literally just "food" for our own sustenance and enjoyment—animals, plants, sun, water, and earth! The world was just a gratuitous painted backdrop so we could do our Christian thing and be "saved"! Yet God created millions of creatures for millions of years before we came along—many of whom we never saw and others of whom we have yet to see or discover—for no human purpose whatsoever. God seems to be concerned to communicate Himself/Herself as endless, multitudinous beauty, love, and fecundity. Almost shocking, isn't it?

For many Judeo-Christians, God had created a seemingly "throw-away world." The so-called "stone age" people, the ancient civilizations, the Persian, Greek, Aztec, Mayan, Inca, and Roman empires, even the poor ones we called barbarians, were merely warm-up acts for us. None of them really mattered to God, neither woman, child, beast, nor man. God was just biding his time, waiting for good Jews, Christians, and Muslims to appear, and most preferably Roman Catholics, conservative Orthodox, or Born-Again Evangelicals.

I am not being unfair here; this is quite literally true. A sort of cosmic narcissism, it seems to me. But if you do not see the individual ego (the separate self) as a problem, it is almost impossible to recognize the corporate separate self as an even worse problem. Thus nationalism, ethnic cleansing of various sorts, burning of heretics, persecution of all that was "not me," including the rest of creation (animals, all growing things, earth, and water), were literally "fair game" for us. Poor God must just cry.

If nothing else, one would have thought good people would be shocked and scandalized at God's gross inefficiency and non-concern for life. But it only got worse, as Christians were assured that all Hindus, Buddhists, Muslims, pagans, atheists, communists, and unbelievers of any stripe (all "not me") were also of no interest whatsoever to their Creator. Apparently, God just likes white Christian Americans, preferably Republican—while this very group wastes not a tear on the fact that their worldview leaves 99 percent of what God has created since the beginning of time lost, rejected, and even punished for all eternity. And this is the group that dares to call itself "pro-life"!

Christians must realize what a muddle we have got ourselves into by not taking incarnation and *the body of God* seriously. It is our only Christian trump card, and we have yet to actually play it! As Sally McFague, a Christian theologian, says so powerfully in her book *The Body of God*, "Salvation is the direction of all of creation, and creation is the very place of salvation." All is God's place, which is our place, which is the only place and every place.

In the fourth century St. Augustine, an official "Doctor of the Church," said that "the church consists in the state of communion of the whole world" (*Ecclesiam in totius orbis communione consistere*). Wherever we are connected, in right relationship—you might say "in love"—there is the Christ, the Body of God, and there is the church, the temple, and the mosque. But Christians sadly whittled that Great Mystery down into something small, exclusive, and manageable too. The church became a Catholic, Orthodox, or Protestant private club, and not necessarily formed by people who were "in communion" with anything else, usually not with the natural world, with non-Christians, or even with other Christians outside their own denomination. It became a very tiny salvation, hardly worthy of the name. God was not magnanimous, or victorious at all, despite all our songs of "How great is our God"!

Our very suffering now, our condensed presence on this common nest that we have largely fouled, will soon be the ONE thing that we finally share in common. It might well be the one thing that will bring us together politically and religiously. The earth and its life systems, on which we all entirely depend (just like God!), might soon become the

very thing that will convert us to a simple lifestyle, to necessary community, and to an inherent and universal sense of
reverence for the Holy. We all breathe the same air and drink
the same water. There are no Jewish, Christian, or Muslim
versions of these universal elements.

I know it is no longer words, doctrines, and mental belief
systems that can or will reveal the fullness of this Cosmic
Christ. This earth indeed is the very Body of God, and it is
from this body that we are born, live, suffer, and resurrect
to eternal life. Either all is God's Great Project, or we may
rightly wonder whether anything is.

> From the beginning until now, the entire creation
> has been groaning in one great act of giving birth,
> and not only creation, but all of us who possess the
> first fruits of the Spirit, we also groan inwardly, as
> we wait for our bodies to be set free.
>
> ROMANS 8:22–23

It seems that St. Paul is saying here that we human ones
might be the last ones to jump aboard God's great plan and
direction. There is the groaning of growing in all of creation,
and the groaning of resisting and "waiting" in all that is
human and animal, and in everything that is forever being
born in new forms, forever growing and dying.

Non-human creation has been obedient to its destiny,
it seems:

> Each mortal thing does one thing and the same:
>   ... *myself* it speaks and spells,
> Crying *What I do is me: for that I came.*
>
> —GERARD MANLEY HOPKINS,
> *"When Kingfishers Catch Fire"*

Wouldn't it be our last and greatest humiliation, surely the "first being last," as Jesus says, if we one day realized that all other creatures have obeyed their destiny unblinkingly and with trustful surrender—all except us? Just watch the plants and animals for even a short while, and you will see their loving obedience. We alone have the "free will" to deny our own destiny.

It is only humans who have resisted "the one great act of giving birth," and in fact have frequently chosen death for themselves and for so many others besides. We can do better, we must do better, and by God's patient grace, we will do better—once we recognize that it is one shared creation and we are all a part of it for better or for worse.

At the level of survival we are fast approaching, our attempts to distinguish ourselves by accidental and historical differences and theological subtleties—while ignoring the clear "bottom line"—are becoming an almost blasphemous waste of time and a shocking disrespect for God's one, beautiful, and multitudinous life. I do still believe that grace is inherent to creation, and that God and goodness will still have the final word.

Dearly beloved!
I have called you so often and you have not heard me.
I have shown myself to you so often
and you have not seen me.
I have made myself fragrance so often,
and you have not smelled me,
Savorous food, and you have not tasted me.
Why can you not reach me through the object you touch
or breathe me through sweet perfumes?
Why do you not see me? Why do you not hear me?
Why? Why? Why?

IBN 'ARABI

Sufi teacher and author LLEWELLYN VAUGHAN-LEE *suggests that we are facing not just an ecological crisis, but a spiritual crisis caused by our deep forgetfulness of the sacred nature of creation. We need to respond to the call of the Earth, begin the work of healing its body and soul. Our present crisis is an opportunity for us to reclaim our sacred role as guardians of the planet.*

The Call of the Earth
LLEWELLYN VAUGHAN-LEE

*The Zen Master Thich Nhat Hanh was once asked
what we need to do to save our world. "What we most
need to do," he replied, "is to hear within us
the sounds of the Earth crying."[1]*

THE CALL

AT THIS MOMENT in time we are more and more consciously confronted by the reality of climate change,
global pollution, acidification of the oceans, massive destruction of forests and wetlands and other natural habitat. All
of it is contributing to the first man-made mass extinction
of species that the planet has suffered, caused by industrialization and our addiction to a materialistic lifestyle. And we
are all responsible—just by traveling in a car or a plane, we are
actively participating in an ecologically destructive culture.

We all need to take responsibility for this pressing
predicament. And although many individuals and groups
have responded, little has really changed in substance on a
collective, governmental level since the 2009 Copenhagen
summit showed us putting short-term economic growth
before the real and lasting concerns of carbon emissions
and climate change.

Moreover, our materialistic culture has co-opted the
concept of sustainability to its own ends. Our collective
objective now appears to be to sustain our materialistic,

energy-intensive way of life, rather than to sustain the ecosystem and its diversity of inhabitants. There are few signs that the world is prepared to give up its materialist pleasures.

And while many people are working to try to counter this imbalance, most are approaching it with the very same mind-set that has created this predicament. Before we can begin to redeem this crisis, we need to go to the root of our present paradigm—our sense of separation from our environment, the lack of awareness that we are all a part of one interdependent living organism that is our planet. This can be traced to the birth of the scientific era in the Age of Enlightenment and the emergence of Newtonian physics, in which humans were seen as separate from the physical world, which in turn was considered as unfeeling matter, a clockwork mechanism whose workings it was our right and duty to understand and control. While this attitude has given us the developments of science and technology, it has severed us from any relationship to the environment as a living whole of whose cycles we are a part. We have lost and entirely forgotten any spiritual relationship to life and the planet, a central reality to other cultures for millennia.[2] Where for indigenous peoples the world was a sacred, inter-connected living whole that cares for us and for which we in turn need to care—our Mother the Earth—for our Western culture it became something to exploit.

And as we move into a global age, it is these Western materialistic values that are dominating more and more of our planet. Our increasingly global consumer-driven civi-lization is amplifying our exploitation and the resulting pollution to an unsustainable level. As the world grows more and more out of balance, we urgently need to regain a relationship with the planet based upon the understanding of the world as a sacred living whole, and to reclaim a con-sciousness that is centered in that understanding. Only if we redeem the problem at its root can we hope to heal and come back into balance with our environment. Would we rape and pillage the physical world if we understood and respected its sacred nature?

But there is an even deeper, and somewhat darker, side to our forgetfulness of the sacred within creation. When our monotheistic religions placed God in heaven they banished the many gods and goddesses of the Earth, of its rivers and mountains. We forgot the ancient wisdom contained in our understanding of the sacred in creation—its rhythms, its meaningful magic. For example, when early Christianity banished paganism and cut down its sacred groves, they forgot about nature *devas*, the powerful spirits and entities within nature, who understand the deeper patterns and properties of the natural world. Now how can we even begin the work of healing the natural world, of clearing out its toxins and pollutants, of bringing it back into balance, if we do not consciously work with these forces within nature? Nature is not unfeeling matter; it is full of invisible forces with their own intelligence and deep knowing. We need to reacknowledge the existence of the spiritual world within creation if we are even to begin the real work of bringing the world back into balance. Only then can we regain the wisdom of the shamans who understood how to communicate and work together with the spirit world.[3]

There has been a recent resurgence in spirituality in the West, what some would call an "awakening." In the last few decades we have been made aware of previously hidden or esoteric techniques and practices to access the spiritual dimension of our self—to reconnect with our soul. Many individuals have followed an inner calling to use these practices and teachings to make a relationship with their soul or spiritual nature. Yet we still have little understanding of the spiritual dimension within the natural world, or of how our individual soul relates to the larger dimension of the world soul (what the ancients called the *anima mundi*). We have mostly lost the knowledge of the spiritual practices and rituals that keep the balance in the inner and outer worlds; we have even forgotten that such practices are needed. Instead we are caught within a contemporary consciousness that focuses on the individual self, no longer even aware of our deep bond to the sacred within creation.

We may have begun to reclaim an understanding of how to relate to our own soul and experienced the meaning and sense of purpose that can come into our life through this relationship. We may even be drawn to spiritual teachings and practices that can help us in this work, that take us beneath the surface of our life into the deeper dimensions of our own being and give us access to the spirit world. Those who have begun to make this journey feel and know the deep nourishment, the guidance that this can bring. We also may have become aware of a certain poverty in our daily life that results from our forgetting this inner reality, the absence of a certain joy or central note. But we have little awareness of the relationship between our individual soul and the world soul. We have forgotten the ancient teaching that says that the individual is the microcosm of the whole, the lesser Adam in relation to the greater Adam that is the whole of creation. We have lost the basic understanding of the ways our spiritual awareness, or our forgetfulness, affects the whole—of the subtle but powerful relationship between human consciousness and our inner and outer environment.

While there may be a growing awareness that the world forms a single living being—what has been called the Gaia principle—we don't really understand that this being is also nourished by its soul, the *anima mundi*—or that we are a part of it, part of a much larger living, sacred being. Sadly we remain cut off, isolated from this spiritual dimension of life itself. We have forgotten how to nourish or be nourished by the soul of the world.[4]

And while there is a growing ecological movement that reminds us that we are guardians of the planet, echoing the religious teaching that we are "vice-regents" (inheritors, *khalifa*) of the Earth,[5] this guardianship is interpreted as looking after our physical environment and its myriad inhabitants, rarely addressing our inherent responsibility of the sacred within creation. Instead, in only relating to our planet from a physical perspective, much of the ecological movement perpetuates the concept of the earth as something solely physical, without sacredness or soul, and so reinforces the divorce of matter from spirit.

While we may remember the sacredness of human beings, we have forgotten that the Earth is also sacred, and that its soul can speak to ours. If we were to understand this dimension of creation, we would realize that our guardianship of the planet means taking responsibility for its physical *and* its sacred nature, and their interrelationship.

This responsibility was always understood by indigenous peoples and their spiritual leaders or shamans. Many of the rituals of daily life as well as their ceremonies and prayers were enacted for the purpose of looking after the sacred nature of creation, keeping the balance between the worlds. For example when the Pomo Indian people of Northern California wove baskets, the women would go out and pray over the grasses before they cut them. As they wove their baskets they would put the reeds or grasses through their mouths to moisten them, praying over them. The basket thus wove together the physical and the spiritual parts of life. All aspects of life were approached in this way, the warp and woof of physical and spiritual woven together into the single fabric of life that was never anything other than sacred. Indigenous peoples saw their life as a communion with earth and spirit that nourished them and at the same time nourished creation, the two being so interwoven it would not have been possible even to think of nourishing the one without nourishing the other.

It is only through awakening to an awareness of the sacred within creation, and of its relationship to our own sacred nature, that we can begin to redeem the primal imbalance that lies at the root of our present predicament. Any awareness of the world as a living whole needs to include its sacred dimension. Otherwise we are just treating the symptoms rather than the cause. We cannot afford to continue the split between spirit and matter—we cannot continue to ignore life's sacred nature.

Whatever our ecological awareness, on a collective level we are living in a materialistic culture that has forgotten the sacred dimension of creation. We have forgotten the existence of the *anima mundi* and the sacred substance within creation that holds the light of its divine nature. It could be suggested that as a result, in our culture daily life has lost much of its sacred meaning and purpose—the deepest joy of being alive. Instead we are more and more caught in the pursuit of surface pleasure and other addictions. We are in the grip of a materialistic culture that focuses only on the physical dimension, whose values are not only destroying our ecosystem but starving our souls.

Furthermore, because we have forgotten this sacred dimension of creation we no longer practice the rituals that nourish it—the simple sacred rituals of daily life that were central to many diverse cultures for millennia. We have also lost the inner attitude of respect for the sacred within creation that in itself was a direct source of communion with the Divine. Instead, our attitude is at best neglect and at worst an abuse of the sacred within creation. The effect of our collective attitude and behavior is that the sacred substance within creation is no longer looked after or nourished by humanity, except for a few indigenous peoples and a few other groups and individuals who still carry and live this responsibility.[6] As a result this sacred substance is becoming less and less accessible, and something within creation and within ourselves is slowly dying. Just as the outer ecosystem is dying, so is the inner spiritual body of the planet. A sacred substance that nourishes our souls and the soul of the world is diminishing. And we do not even know that this is happening.

Because we have collectively forgotten the sacred dimension to all of life, we have lost the awareness that this sacred dimension nourishes our own soul, and that we need to relate to it. We no longer know how to listen to the voice of the world soul, how to read its signs. When we witnessed the oil spill in the Gulf of Mexico, did we dare to read the book of life and see what this worst ecological disaster in North America was telling us? What was the deeper meaning of this disaster as the flow of oil met the flow of the water, as our most fundamental resource and all the life that depended upon it was being toxically contaminated by our need or greed for oil?

We remain unaware of how our forgetfulness affects both the world and our own self. Our neglect and dismissal of the sacred within creation are creating an inner wasteland as real as the Tar Sands in Alberta. The globalization of our soulless, materialistic culture is having disastrous effects in the inner world, polluting it as much as the outer environment. And like the danger of climate change and extinction of species, this inner wasteland is growing faster than we realize.

Our collective forgetfulness of the sacred in creation is beginning to have an effect as irreversible and catastrophic as climate change. In fact one could say that this outer, physical predicament is a reflection of an inner catastrophe —a catastrophe that is even more disastrous because we remain unaware of it.[7]

We may not be consciously aware of what is happening, yet many people feel it deep within. There is a primal anxiety beneath the surface of our Western material abundance. We may project this anxiety onto the outer political or economic situation, but there is a sense that something vital to life is being lost.[8]

The most direct and disastrous effect of that loss, our loss of the sacred, is that the soul of humanity and the soul of the world will lose their sacred meaning and purpose. We are a part of the world, of its spiritual as well as its physical body, and it is the sacred that alone can give deep meaning to the individual and to the whole. What the loss of this sacred substance within creation as a whole could mean we do not know, except that any sense of meaning or purpose to life beyond that of physical survival or material enjoyment will grow less and less accessible. We will all find ourselves more and more caught in the surface fractures of existence, in our addictions and distractions, and less and less in touch with life's primal joy and underlying unity. The real purpose of our soul will become more and more obscured. Sometimes in an individual one can glimpse how through drugs or other addictions a certain light in the eyes, the light of the soul, has gone dull, even gone out. Such people have lost their way in a life that no longer has access to its purpose. Could this happen to the whole of humanity, could this light in the world soul be dimmed, even extinguished? And what would this mean to the world itself?

We may see in the outer world the effects of our ego-driven materialistic culture, and, in our ecological crisis, may be beginning to wake up to its danger. But the effects on the inner world remain veiled, hidden by our very forgetfulness of the inner world and its sacred nature—our rational culture's denial of its very existence. All that is sure is that an inner tragedy as potent as climate change is taking place—the inner and outer life reflect each other more than we know. We are losing what is most sacred to life, what gives existence real meaning and purpose. And yet our forgetfulness of the sacred nature of creation itself means that we do not realize what is happening. Maybe this is the greatest tragedy—that it remains unnoticed, unacknowledged.

THE RESPONSE

How do we respond to such a hidden crisis? How can we awaken from our dream of forgetfulness? If we have a sense that something deep within our being, and within the being of the world, is out of balance, we can listen. We then may hear the cry of the world, its call to us. This is not just the call of creation as its physical ecosystem is being destroyed, but the cry of the world soul, the anguish of the *anima mundi* as it feels its sacred substance being depleted, its light going out.

And from hearing this cry we might begin to awaken, to sense a lack of the sacred, of this primal substance that gives meaning to all of life. We will each hear this cry in our own way, as it touches our own soul, but what matters is how we respond—whether we turn away, returning to our life of distractions, or whether we dare to follow the call and sense what it is telling us. Then, for an instant, we might catch a fragrance that is vanishing, a color that is fading. We might begin to notice what is happening.

In the outer world the signs are all around us. Daily we see the physical signs of our ecological crisis: the glaciers melting, the floods and droughts. We may also sense the deep anxiety of a civilization that has lost its way, forgotten its primal connection to the sacred that alone can give real meaning. If we are to take real responsibility for our present predicament we need to respond both outwardly and inwardly. We need to work to heal both the body and the soul of the world.

The first step is always to recognize what is happening. We can no longer afford to be blinkered by the surface values of our materialistic culture. Just as real sustainability embraces the biodiversity of the whole planet, it also includes the sacred within creation. We need to relearn the wisdom of listening to life, feeling its heartbeat, sensing its soul. But first there is a pressing need to reconnect matter and spirit. All of life is sacred, every breath and every stone. This is one of the great secrets of oneness—everything is included. Within our heart and soul we can reconnect with our primal knowing that the Divine is present in everything.

We cannot return to the simplicity of an indigenous lifestyle, but we can become aware that what we do and how we are at an individual level affects the global environment, both outer and inner. We can learn how to live in a more sustainable way, not to be drawn into unnecessary materialism. We can also work to heal the spiritual imbalance in the world. Our individual conscious awareness of the sacred within creation reconnects the split between spirit and matter within our own soul and also within the soul of the world: we are part of the spiritual body of the Earth more than we know.

We will each have our own way of making this offering. There is, for example, a simple prayer for the Earth: the act of placing the world as a living being within our hearts when we inwardly remember the Divine. We become aware in our hearts of the sorrow and suffering of the world, and ask that divine love and healing flow where needed. And through our prayers the power of the Divine will help us and help the world—help to bring the Earth back into balance. We need to remember that the power of the Divine is more than that of all the global corporations that continue to make the world a wasteland, even more than the global forces of consumerism that demand the lifeblood of the planet. We need to reawaken to the power of love in the world.

Sometimes it is easier to feel this connection when we feel the earth in our hands, when we work in the garden tending our flowers or vegetables. Or when we cook, preparing the vegetables that the earth has given us, mixing in the herbs and spices that provide flavor. Making love, as we share our body and bliss with our lover, we may feel the tenderness and power of creation, how a single spark can give birth. Then our lovemaking can be an offering to life itself, a fully felt remembrance of the ecstasy of creation.

The divine oneness of life is within and all around us. Sometimes walking alone in nature we can feel its heartbeat and its wonder, and our steps become steps of remembrance. The simple practice of "walking in a sacred manner"—in which with every step we take we feel the connection with the sacred Earth—is one way to reconnect with the living spirit of the Earth.

There are so many ways to reconnect with the sacred within creation, to listen within and include the Earth in our spiritual practice and daily life. When we hear the morning chorus of birds, we may sense that deeper joy of life and awake to its divine nature; at night the stars can remind us of what is infinite and eternal within us and within the world. Watching the simple wonder of a dawn or a sunset can be an offering in itself. Whatever way we are drawn to wonder, to recognize the sacred, what matters is always the attitude we bring to this intimate exchange. It is through the heart that a real connection is made, even if we first make it in our feet or hands. Do we really feel our self as a part of this beautiful and suffering planet, do we sense its need? Then this connection comes alive, a living stream that flows from our heart as it embraces all of life. Then every step, every touch, will be a prayer for the Earth, a remembrance of what is sacred.

Our present ecological crisis is calling to us and it is for each of us to respond. This crisis is not a problem to be solved, because the world is not a problem but a living being in a state of dangerous imbalance and deep distress. This distress belongs to its body and soul, and as the voices in this book show, there are different ways we can respond to this calling. What matters is how through our own response we reconnect to what is sacred, and return to a sense of deep belonging, here in this place of wonder we call the Earth.

There is action to be taken in the outer world, but it must be action that comes from a reconnection with the sacred— otherwise we will just be reconstellating the patterns that have created this imbalance. And there is work to be done within our hearts and souls, the foundational work of healing the soul of the world, of replenishing the spiritual substance of creation—of bringing the healing power of divine love and remembrance where it is most needed. The crisis we face now is dire, but it is also an opportunity for humanity to reclaim its role as guardian of the planet, to take responsibility for the wonder and mystery of this living, sacred world.

Epilogue
A FINAL PRAYER

WITHIN all these different voices is one voice and one story, the story of the Earth that needs our attention and prayers, that needs our love and support, as much as it has always given us the love and support we need. May we remember our role as guardians of the Earth, custodians of its sacred ways, and return once again to live in harmony with its natural rhythms and laws.

Notes

THOMAS BERRY

1. Margulis, Lynn, and Sagan, Dorion, *Microcosmos: Four Billion Years of Microbial Evolution,* (Berkeley: University of California Press 1997), p. 191.
2. Teilhard de Chardin, Pierre, *The Human Phenomenon,* trans. Sarah Appleton-Weber, (Eastbourne, East Sussex: Sussex Academic Press, 1999), p. 3.
3. Thoreau, Henry David, *Walking: A Little Book of Wisdom,* (New York: Harper Collins, 1994), p. 19. This was originally published as the essay "Walking" in *Atlantic Monthly,* after Thoreau's death in 1862.

CHIEF TAMALE BWOYA

1. For a longer description of this vision, including images, visit: www.spiritualecology.org/article/revelation-laikipia-kenya.

MARY EVELYN TUCKER & BRIAN THOMAS SWIMME

1. Crutzen, P.J., The effects of industrial and agricultural practices on atmospheric chemistry and climate during the Anthropocene, *Journal of Environmental Science and Health,* Part A 37, 423–424 (2002).
2. Christian, D., *Maps of Time: An Introduction to Big History,* (Berkeley: University of California Press, 2005).
3. Brown, C.S., *Big History: From the Big Bang to the Present,* (New York: New Press, 2007).
4. Great Transition Initiative [online], www.gtinitiative.org.
5. Macy, J., *The Great Turning,* (Berkeley: Center for Ecoliteracy, 2007).
6. Layard, R., *Happiness: Lessons from a New Science,* (New York: Penguin, 2006).
7. Journey of the Universe [online], www.journeyoftheuniverse.org.
8. Hawken, P., *Blessed Unrest: How the Largest Social Movement in History Is Restoring Grace, Justice, and Beauty to the World,* (New York: Penguin, 2008).
9. Wilson, E.O., *Consilience: The Unity of Knowledge,* (New York: Vintage, 1999).
10. Chaisson, E.J., *Cosmic Evolution: The Rise of Complexity in Nature,* (Cambridge, MA: Harvard University Press, 2002).

11. Steffen, W., Rockström, J., & Costanza, R., How defining planetary boundaries can transform our approach to growth, *Solutions* [online] 2(3) (May 2011), www.thesolutionsjournal.com/node/935.
12. Christian, D., Big history for the era of climate change. *Solutions* [online] 3(2) (March 2012), www.thesolutionsjournal.com/node/1066.

WENDELL BERRY

1. *Another Turn of the Crank*, p. 89.

VANDANA SHIVA

1. Taittiriya Upanishad, 2.2, trans. Robert Ernest Hume, *The Thirteen Principal Upanishads*, 2nd English Ed., Oxford University Press.
2. Ibid 3–2, p. 290.
3. Ibid 2.2, p. 284.
4. Maha Ashwamedhika, 92.

SATISH KUMAR

1. *Talks on the Gita*, Paramdham Prakashan, Pavnar, Warda, India, ch. 9, p. 124.
2. Ibid., ch. 10, p. 153.
3. Ibid., ch. 17, p. 241.
4. Ibid., ch. 17, p. 242.

GENEEN MARIE HAUGEN

1. De Quincy, Christian, *Radical Nature: Redeeming the Soul of Matter*, (Montpelier, VT: Inner Cities Press, 2002), pp. 42–43.
2. Hillman, James, *The Thought of the Heart and the Soul of the World*, (Putnam, CT: Spring Publications, 1992), pp. 22–23.
3. Berry, Thomas, *Evening Thoughts: Reflecting on Earth as Sacred Community*, ed. Mary Evelyn Tucker, (San Francisco: Sierra, 2006), p. 57.
4. Tarnas, Richard, *Cosmos and Psyche: Intimations of a New Worldview*, (New York: Viking, 2006), p. 39.
5. Hillman, p. 102.

JULES CASHFORD

1. Cashford, Jules, trans., *The Homeric Hymns* (Penguin Classics, 2003); quoted in *Gaia, from Story of Origin to Universe Story*, (London: Gaia Press, 2010).
2. Shakespeare, *A Midsummer Night's Dream*, V, i, 15–16.
3. *The Gospel According to Thomas*, Coptic Text est. and trans. by A. Guillaumont et al. (Leiden: E. J. Brill, 1976), passim.
4. Plato, *The Timaeus*, 29/30.
5. Chief Seattle, quoted in Anne Baring and Jules Cashford, *The Myth of the Goddess: Evolution of an Image*, (London: Penguin, 1992), p. 681.
6. Yeats, W. B., *Essays and Introductions*, (London: Macmillan Press Ltd., 1961), passim, especially pp. 50–52.
7. Lovelock, James, *Gaia: A New Look at Life on Earth*, (Oxford: OUP, 1979).
8. Rilke, R.M., *Letters to a Young Poet*, trans. M.D. Herter Norton (New York & London: W.W. Norton & Co.), p. 38.
9. Coleridge, S.T., *The Statesman's Manual*, (New York: Harcourt Brace Jovanovich), p. 476.
10. See P. B. Shelley, *A Defence of Poetry*, ll. 111–113.
11. Hesiod, *Theogony*, trans. Dorothea Wender, in *Hesiod and Theognis*, (London: Penguin Classics, 1973), pp. 27–9.
12. See Baring and Cashford, *The Myth of the Goddess*, ch. 14.
13. Jung, *The Tavistock Lectures*, p. 682.
14. Rilke, "To Music."
15. Campbell, Joseph, *The Inner Reaches of Outer Space: Metaphor as Myth and Religion*, (New York: Alfred van der Marck Editions and Toronto: St. James's Press Ltd., 1986), p. 17.
16. Einstein, Albert, *The Expanded Quotable Einstein*, ed. Alice Calaprice, (Princeton and Oxford: Princeton University Press, 2000), p. 316.

BILL PLOTKIN

1. The first three definitions of Soul in this sentence are from poet David Whyte. The final one is from Geneen Marie Haugen.
2. For many more examples, all with much greater elaboration, see my books *Soulcraft: Crossing into the Mysteries of Nature and Psyche*, (New World Library, 2003) and *Nature and the Human Soul: Cultivating Wholeness and Community in a Fragmented World*, (New World Library, 2008).

3. From "The Song of Wandering Aengus," in *The Collected Poems of W.B. Yeats*, ed. Richard J. Finneran, (New York: Scribner, 1996), p. 59.

4. Macy, Joanna, *Widening Circles*, (Gabriola Island, BC: New Society Publishers, 2000), p. 106. Also see *Nature and the Human Soul*, pp. 269–271, for a discussion of this and a second of Joanna's encounters with soul.

5. Berry, Thomas, *The Great Work*, (New York: Bell Tower, 1999), p. 13, and *The Dream of the Earth*, (San Francisco: Sierra Club Books, 1988).

6. See *Nature and the Human Soul*.

7. Jeffers, Robinson, from "De Rerum Virtute" in *The Wild God of the World*, (Palo Alto: Stanford University Press, 2003), p. 176.

8. I explore ecocentric-soulcentric child development in some detail in chapters four and five of *Nature and the Human Soul*.

9. Berry, Thomas, *Every Being Has Rights*, (Great Barrington, MA: E. F. Schumacher Society, 2004), p. 7.

10. See *Soulcraft* and *Nature and the Human Soul* for in-depth descriptions of the process of soul initiation.

11. Macy, Joanna, and Young Brown, Molly, *Coming Back to Life: Practices to Reconnect Our Lives, Our World*, (Gabriola Island, BC: New Society Publishers, 1998), p. 135.

12. Berry, *Every Being Has Rights*, p. 9.

13. From the Earth Charter website, www.earthcharter.org: "Created by the largest global consultation process ever associated with an international declaration, endorsed by thousands of organizations representing millions of individuals, the Earth Charter seeks to inspire in all peoples a sense of global interdependence and shared responsibility for the well-being of the human family and the larger living world." The drafting of the Earth Charter was catalyzed by the 1992 Earth Summit held in Rio de Janeiro. As of November 2012, the United Nations has not yet endorsed the Earth Charter. However, the Earth Charter International Council is spearheading the effort to persuade the U.N. to do so, as well as engaging in many other projects to raise awareness about the charter and increase engagement with the principles and practice of sustainable development.

14. Joanna Macy, personal communication, 2007.

PIR ZIA INAYAT KHAN

1. West, W.E., trans., *Pahlavi Texts*, part V (Delhi: Motilal Banarsidass, 1987), p. 161.
2. Darmesteter, James, trans., *The Zenda-Avesta*, part II (Delhi: Motilal Banarsidass, 1981), p. 229.
3. Zu'l-'ulum Azar Kayvan, *Jam-i Kay Khusraw*, (Bombay: Matba'-yi Fazl al-Din Kahamkar, 1868), pp. 10–12.
4. Ibid.
5. Mawlana Jalal al-Din Rumi, *Masnavi-yi ma'navi*, (Tehran: Intisharat-i Bihnud, 1954), p. 36.
6. Vamana Purana 12:26, quoted in Christopher Key Chapple, "Hinduism and Deep Ecology," in David L. Barnhill and Roger S. Gottlieb, eds., *Deep Ecology and World Religions*, (Albany: State University of New York Press, 2001), p. 61.
7. Khwaja Mu'in al-Din Chishti, *Risala-yi sarmaya-yi yug*, (personal MS), folio 2a-b.
8. Imam al-Salikin Muhammad Taqi Niyazi ('Aziz Miyan), *Raz-i muhabbat*, (Bareilly, U.P.: Shamsi Press, n.d.), pp. 46–48.
9. Hazrat Inayat Khan, *The Sufi Message*, Vol. XI, (London: Barrie and Jenkins, 1964), p. 41.
10. Hazrat Inayat Khan, *Complete Works: Sayings*, Part I, (The Hague: East-West Publications, 1989), p. 198.
11. Dastur Framroze Bode and Piloo Nanavutty, trans., *Songs of Zarathushtra*, (London: George Allen & Unwin, 1952), p. 46 (modified).

LLEWELLYN VAUGHAN-LEE

1. Quoted in Joanna Macy and Molly Young Brown, *Coming Back to Life: Practices to Reconnect Our Lives, Our World*, (Gabriola Island, BC: New Society Publishers, 1998), p. 91.
2. In earlier times the symbolic world permeated daily life and the physical world, as can be seen in the iconography of the Gothic cathedrals, while in the Middle Ages and earlier the image of the Great Chain of Being imaged all the "levels" of creation linked together, from God and the angels to the animals and minerals.
3. The work of the Findhorn Foundation in Scotland began with relearning how to communicate and work with the forces within nature, the devas and nature spirits.
4. Carl Jung describes this tragedy: "Man himself has ceased to be the microcosm and his anima is no longer the consubstantial

      scintilla or spark of the *Anima Mundi*, the World Soul." (*Collected Works*, vol. 11, ¶ 759.) For a fuller exploration of the *anima mundi* and its history see Vaughan-Lee, *Return of the Feminine and the World Soul*, ch. 8: Anima Mundi.

5.   Qur'an, (*Sūra* 35:39): "He it is that has made you vice-regent in the earth." In the Bible God gives mankind "dominion" over creation (Genesis 1:26): "And God said, Let us make man in our image, after our likeness: and let them have dominion over the fish of the sea, and over the fowl of the air, and over the cattle, and over all the earth, and over every creeping thing that creepeth upon the earth." But it is worth noting that the Jewish tradition equates dominion with guardianship.

6.   For example, the Kogi, an indigenous people living in the Sierra Nevada de Santa Marta mountains of northern Colombia, in Central America. They describe the inner spirit realm or world soul as "Aluna," and through deep meditation and symbolic offerings, the Kogi priests, or Mamas, believe they sustain the balance of harmony and creativity in the world.

7.   There is a body of spiritual teachings that suggests that the inner and outer worlds reflect each other, are "interdependent fields of experience." Some say that any change in the outer world originates in the inner, as expressed by the saying, "All change comes from within." Thus if we are to effect any real change in the outer environment, we must first change the inner.

8.   Is it just a coincidence that the most popular teenage fiction is about vampires and zombies? Or could these young people sense a bleakness to their future: that the life blood of the planet is being lost, that we are facing the danger of a life without real meaning, of becoming the living dead?

Acknowledgments

For permission to use copyrighted material, the author gratefully wishes to acknowledge: Parallax Press, for permission to reprint "The Greening of the Self," an excerpt from *World As Lover, World As Self*, by Joanna Macy, Copyright ©1991, and also for permission to reprint "The Bells of Mindfulness," an excerpt from *The World We Have: A Buddhist Approach to Peace and Ecology*, by Thich Nhat Hanh, Copyright ©2008, Parallax Press, Berkeley, California, www.parallax.org; Columbia University Press, for permission to reprint "The World of Wonder," an excerpt from *The Sacred Universe* by Thomas Berry, Copyright ©2009 Columbia University Press; and Liveright Publishing Corporation, for permission to use the lines from "i thank You God for most this amazing," Copyright 1950, ©1978, 1991 by the Trustees for the E. E. Cummings Trust, Copyright ©1979 by George James Firmage, from *Complete Poems: 1904–1962 by E. E. Cummings*, edited by George J. Firmage.

About the Publisher

THE GOLDEN SUFI CENTER publishes books, video, and audio on Sufism, mysticism, and the awakening consciousness of oneness. A California religious nonprofit 501(c)(3) corporation, it is dedicated to making the teachings of the Naqshbandi Sufi path available to all seekers. For further information about activities and publications, please contact:

THE GOLDEN SUFI CENTER
P.O. Box 456
Point Reyes Station, CA 94956-0456
tel: 415-663-0100 · *fax:* 415-663-0103
www.goldensufi.org

About Spiritual Ecology
www.spiritualecology.org

"If we are to restore the balance in our world,
we need to go beneath the surface to heal the
split between spirit and matter and help
to bring the sacred back into life."

LLEWELLYN VAUGHAN-LEE

Spiritual Ecology is an exploration of the spiritual
dimension of our present ecological crisis. In
particular the resources available through this website
explore the relationship between our outer, physical
ecological situation, our awareness of the sacred in
creation, and our inner relationship to the symbolic
world of the soul—and how this affects our own soul
and the soul of the world, the *anima mundi*.